2ND Edition

Marketing the One-Person Business

Mike Rounds and Nancy Miller

Marketing the One-Person Business
Mike Rounds and Nancy Miller

Published by:

SYSTEMS
PUBLISHING COMPANY
6318 Ridgepath Court
Rancho Palos Verdes, CA 90275-3248
mailto:CPMSystems@RoundsMiller.com

This book is written with the understanding that the authors were not engaged in rendering legal services. The information included has been carefully prepared and is correct to the best of our knowledge as of the publication date. If you require legal or expert advice, the services of professionals should be used. The authors disclaim any personal liability, either directly or indirectly, for advice or information presented in this book.

The information as described herein has been used successfully to obtain profitable business for some of the people who have used it. Although all efforts have been expended to supply you with the latest in complete, accurate and up-to-date information, it must be understood that the ultimate success of the user is dependent upon market conditions, efforts expended by the user, and other variable factors that are beyond the control of the authors, and that neither the user's actual expenses nor profits are guaranteed nor implied.

Throughout this book, trademarked names are used. Rather than put a trademark symbol after every occurrence of the trademarked name, we use the names in an editorial fashion only, and to the benefit of the trademark owner, with no intentions of infringement of the trademark.

This book contains excerpted copyrighted material from "Mechanics of Mail Order Second Edition" by Nancy Miller and Mike Rounds included in Chapter 5, and "How to Sell Your Inventions for Cash Second Edition" by Mike Rounds, included in Chapter 4's agreements, and Chapter 12 both published by CPM Systems. Chapter 11 "A Speaker's Web Site" was previously copyrighted by Mike Rounds. The sample speaker's one-sheet on page 109-110 is copyrighted by Sheryl Roush and included in this book with her permission.

Cover design by http://www.beitnow.com

ISBN 1-891440-29-2

Printed in the United State of America
First Printing, 2004
Copyright © 1998 and 2004 by Michael F. Rounds and Nancy Miller

Library of Congress Cataloging-in-Publication Data

Rounds, Mike.
   Marketing the one-person business / Mike Rounds and Nancy Miller.-- 2nd ed.
        p. cm.
   Includes bibliographical references and index.
   ISBN 1-891440-29-2
 1. Marketing. 2. Small business--Marketing. 3. Self-employed. 4. New business
enterprises. 5. Small business--Management. I. Miller, Nancy, 1958- II. Title.

   HF5415.R639 2004
   658.8--dc22

                                                            2004019950

Table of Contents

iv

Other Products Available

Clutterology® Getting Rid of Clutter and Getting Organized! book, videotape and VCD

Creating Low-Cost High-Profit Products videotape and VCD

Fishin' With A Net 6th Edition book

How To Sell Your Inventions For Cash 2nd Edition book

Marketing with Postcards videotape and VCD

Professional Speaker's Marketing Handbook e-book

Talk Talk Talk Speaker's Success Stories videotape

Clueless Series:
> Boothmanship
> Inventing
> Patents
> Project Management
> Self-Publishing
> Telemarketing
> Trademark and Copyright
> Venture Capital

Consulting services

Order these and more on-line at http://www.RoundsMiller.com

Chapter 1 What Is The One-Person Business?

America has over 15.7 million one-person businesses accounting for over $643 billion in receipts annually according to a report from the U.S. Census Bureau. Technically, a one-person business is any business that has a single employee (that's you) doing all of the work. This could be a manufacturing business that deals in small-scale production, but more likely it's an individual who is selling services to a client.

The two operative words are service and selling—both of which are important to the success of the business. Let's examine services and selling a little more closely.

What is a service? A service is either providing labor and/or the information to achieve an objective or goal. For many of us, this service is called consulting, which is: any service that provides labor, knowledge or information and does not require that the person be captive to any single employer or contract.

If we use this definition, we've just described lawyers and plumbers. The difference is that one provides a service and the other provides manual labor.

The second word is sales—that dreaded and repulsive word that automatically conjures up mental images of a door-to-door peddler with a vacuum cleaner in one hand and a contract in the other—selling.

Actually, you're all in sales and you're selling all the time—you just don't call it sales. If you invite friends to lunch and they accept, you've sold them on being in your company for the occasion. If you present a report and your peers accept it, you've sold them on your credibility.

Selling (or more correctly—marketing) is anything you do to get or keep clients. Selling is nothing more than getting other people to see and do things your way. It's that simple and that complicated—all at the same time.

Now, here's why it's so important to the one-person business: individuals who are good at what they do create one-person businesses. That's why you went into business in the first place.

Your business, like all other businesses, has two parts:

1. Doing the business.

2. Getting the business (this means sales).

Given the choice between doing the business and getting the business, you would probably rather do the business than get the business. Why? Because you're good at the business and know how to do it and keep it doing what it's supposed to be doing.

The problem arises when sales are ignored, and this generally happens because the person running the business is good at the functional side of it. The getting (sales) isn't always fun. You must put yourself out in front of people and ask them if they want to hire you. It requires being outgoing and proactive. They could say no! It's far less controllable than doing the business.

In order to be successful, the single person who owns and operates a business MUST spend a calculated percentage of time getting the business that you are good at doing, or shortly you will run out of business to do.

CONSULTING

Once upon a time, consulting was a dirty word. Many people felt that the only reason you would want to be a consultant was because you were unemployable or that you were between jobs. Until the mid-1970s, this might have been true for many professions, but today it's the exact opposite.

When the industrial revolution hit the world in the late 1800s, many people went to work for somebody else. They would go to a predefined location, perform a predefined series of tasks, start and finish at a predetermined time, collect their checks for a predetermined amount, and live predetermined lives as defined by their employer.

Consultants were an oddity because what they did was not predefined in any conventional sense of the word. In fact, they were blatantly independent. Consultants became a source of trouble for the regular employees.

Companies would never consider using a consultant unless something was wrong that management didn't want to fix, or didn't know how to fix. They needed a consultant to come in and remedy the problem for them. In fact, the process was called chainsaw consulting because the consultant usually ended up creating a report that recommended cutting a number of employees.

By hiring an outside specialist to do the research, create the report, and make the recommendations, middle and upper management kept their hands clean of the process and were not considered the bad guys to the employees who remained. This clean hands philosophy was considered to be a moral imperative if management wanted to continue to elicit any degree of loyalty from the remainder of the work force. After all, it was that nasty consultant who made them get rid of friends and co-workers, not them. Management was simply following the dictates and guidelines of the company who ordered them to hire the consultant and follow the recommendations given.

Even though there is still a degree of chainsaw consulting, consulting is useful, productive, legitimate, and an integral part of the business plans of many organizations.

Utilizing consulting services, rather than employing full-time employees operates many of today's businesses more successfully and profitably. In fact, many new businesses are now planned and created with the concept of using contract labor and services, rather than planning on a full-time work force— it's simply more efficient from a time and financial standpoint.

Financial expediency has pushed the consultant to the forefront of the labor market and rightly so because a consultant is paid for performance—not for presence. Consultants help achieve goals through:

- Consulting, advising, and designing programs to fill the gaps between the actual situation and the desired one.

- Coaching, guiding, and training (different levels).

- Developing management and supervisory skills and know-how.

- Defining the company's mission, goals, and objectives.

- Assessing the actual situation.

- Identifying training and operational needs.

- Improving organizational communications.

- Improving work performance.

- Increasing employee motivation.

- Raising the levels of organizational performance and achievements.

- Achieving customer satisfaction and customer loyalty.

- Enlarging the company's customer base and market segment.

FINANCIAL JUSTIFICATION

According to American Demographics Magazine, the average middle management employee:

- Is paid $60,000 per year.

- Requires an additional 30 percent payout in employers' contributions.

- Ends up costing the employer $78,000 per year regardless of the competency of the work performed.

The same study showed that these same individuals:

- Are used for management functions that does not contribute to the bottom-line profits.

- Consequently have an average of 40 percent affectivity in contributing to the bottom-line profits.

- End up costing the employer $78,000 for $31,000 worth of productive work.

- File personal injury, workers compensation, sexual harassment, and wrongful termination suits that cost the employer upward of an additional 10 to 20 percent of gross salary each year.

After carefully weighing the financial and emotional elements involved, many businesses have found that it is far more expedient to contract directly with a consultant rather than to hold a management employee on staff full time:

- For a fixed price.

- For a specified amount of time.

- For a guaranteed level of performance.

This is a radical departure from the old days when consultants were hired only as scapegoats. What changed? Did management suddenly become enlightened to the financial expediency of paying for performance rather than someone's presence?

Did consultants suddenly become infused with the wisdom of the ages so that they can now effectively perform the duties of middle management where before they could not?

Not at all—in fact, business owners have known for a long time that the functional aspects of the business would be much better served by contracting for the services. After all, the process isn't new. For years businesses have made make or buy decisions based on whether it was more expedient to build something in-house or to buy it from an outside supplier. Now it's being applied to all facets of labor and technology.

What changed was the ability of business to replace the 60 percent of what middle management does—monitor, compile, and report on what the work force and productive elements of the organization are doing. When computers started to proliferate in the business world, the monitoring, compiling, and reporting functions became automated to the point where the middle management employees were considered to be extra baggage and were phased out.

However, the need for the 40 percent actual work that the middle managers performed still remained, so instead of hiring a full-time employee to work 40 percent of the time, organizations are now utilizing consultants to perform those tasks as required.

Consultants are hired to replace the actual work that middle management used to perform—not the supervisory functions.

WHAT ARE YOU?

Whether you call yourself a consultant or not may determine not only what you are expected to do but whether or not you'll be hired at all. Because of the colloquial interpretations of words and titles, different names have come to denote different expectations on the part of the client. Calling yourself one thing or another represents a different set of expectations.

Here are the four titles and the descriptions of the works that most clients will expect you to perform:

1. A consultant, by definition actually does the work for the client. For example, if you are a graphic design consultant, the client will expect you to actually create the finished designs for them.

2. A coach imparts or transfers knowledge and/or processes and then works with the client to apply what was transferred. A person who teaches group yoga and breathing techniques and then monitors and corrects the attendee's performance is a good example.

3. A trainer transfers knowledge to the client, their staff, or their employees and bears no responsibility for its application or usage. Anyone who lectures about a topic or teaches a skill is a trainer.

4. A facilitator works with a client to extract the knowledge and skills that are enclosed within the staff and management so that they can be effectively applied to the current needs of the organization or project. For example, if you attend a management retreat there will probably be a facilitator that will *probe* the attendees for ideas that can be applied to help the organization grow and prosper.

One of the most common questions asked is: "What's the difference between a coach and a consultant?"

The answer lies in the definitions of what they do, as shown above, but the primary difference is that a consultant does everything as a customized response to the client's requirements whereas a coach usually has a predefined set of criteria that they expect the client to follow.

If you find that there is some level of overlap between the information don't be alarmed—you'll probably be applying all of the elements at one time or another in your career even though you label yourself as one of the primary titles shown above.

GETTING HIRED

Understanding the motivation for hiring consultants will help you shape the approach you take in selling your services. The approach taken here is termed client driven selling because identifying the prospect's needs is foremost.

The four-step hierarchy for considering your skills is as follows:

1. Area of expertise. Obviously you must be skilled in the area of need the client has defined.

2. Reputation. Clients prefer to hire the best and most reputable individual in the area that they have defined.

3. Fees. Regardless of individuals who tell you that *the money doesn't count*, it does in certain situations. Obviously, clients don't want to pay more than they have to for the services they require but more importantly there are times, places, situations, and cases where skills are shopped as a commodity and the lowest bidder who complies gets the work.

4. Availability. Since you are not a captive employee, your schedule of availability determines whether or not you'll be available when the needs for your services arise.

As you might suspect, there is no single reason consultants are hired. What follows is a list of the many possible reasons. Which reasons apply to hiring you, given the consultancy you are thinking of creating? The reason for exploring them has to do with how you present and market yourself. As you look at each reason, know that each one presents a different set of challenges and opportunities—each one requiring a different approach to selling your services.

Put a check next to each one that may apply to your consulting practice:

☐   The skills needed are not available within the organization. Outside help is the only way to get the skills needed to solve the problem or complete the project.

☐   In-house people don't have time. Even if the organization has the expertise for the project, in-house staff cannot take time away from their regular work.

☐   Organizations want a fresh perspective on their problem or business. Organizations want the new ideas only an outsider can provide, or they want an independent, unbiased point of view.

☐   The prospect cannot identify what needs to be done. I can provide an objective assessment of a situation and help define the problem.

☐   I may be faster and more cost effective than in-house staff. I may have worked on a similar project and can often do it faster and more skillfully than in-house staff, and sometimes at a lower cost.

☐   I can provide a second opinion. In-house approaches often miss the mark because the staff is too close to the problem.

☐   I allow flexibility in staffing. When the project ends, the organization can end the consulting relationship easily and quickly. There is no long-term obligation, or concern about wrongful discharge suits.

Keep in mind the following regarding hiring and using consultants:

1. The clients do not care about what you do.

2. The clients do not care how you do it.

3. The clients do care about what it is that you do for them.

This has to do with an acronym called WIIFM—What's In It For Me? WIIFT—What's In It For Them?

When you're selling services, always consider WIIFM and WIIFT. What these mean is that people buy based on their needs and values, not on yours.

No matter how valuable you believe what you're offering is worth, if you do not impart that same value to somebody else, they're not going to buy your services.

Your clients will be buying your services based on their needs, so they're concerned about the benefits of hiring you instead of using a full-time employee or doing it themselves. Although clients have reasons for hiring you, the real motivation is the benefits they believe they will receive when your tasks are completed.

People buy drills (a product) to get holes (the benefit) and until somebody comes up with Velcro stick-on holes, we'll continue to purchase a product we don't want or care about to get a benefit that's important to us.

Consulting has six major benefit categories. Examine the following information carefully and decide which of the six, or combination of them, you will be offering a client. It is your responsibility to promote these benefits in everything you do because this is what people are buying when they hire you as a consultant.

1. Profit or gain. The client believes that they're going to materially profit, or that their financial situation or their material worth is going to improve by buying whatever it is that you're offering. This is any service that will make money, save money or save time. Examples would be:

    •   Make money—marketing and sales consultants.

    •   Save money—CFP, CPA, and financial analysts.

    •   Save time—project management, and organizational specialists.

2. Fear of loss. People are afraid of losing what they already have. Examples of these services are insurance specialists and security (burglar alarm) experts.

3. Pleasure. We purchase some services simply because we say, "I like it, I want it, I deserve it; therefore, I'm going to get it." An example of pleasure services is a personal trainer. It's an option that people want and people pay more for what they want than what they need.

4. Avoidance of pain. Also defined as anything that makes or appears to make life easier for the client. This is the PRIMARY reason why consultants are hired—to make life easier for the client. Examples would be hiring an accountant to do the taxes you would struggle with yourself, or hiring an interior decorator rather than spending countless hours trying to learn what colors and patterns will look best.

5. Pride. We take pride in who we are, what we do, and how our friends, neighbors, and family perceive us. Some interesting examples of pride are color classes, modeling lessons, and the things we do to improve our personal appearance. Pride is the primary reason why people have their automobiles repainted. A car does not run better with the rust spots sanded out, but because we take pride in how we're perceived by our friends and neighbors, we have our car repainted.

6. Approval. Peer group approval, family approval, and business associate approval are defined as approval. One service in this area is graphic design. A small business starting out doesn't want to look like a newcomer to the industry, so a graphic design consultant is hired to create an appearance of long standing success and service to the industry. By creating this appearance, you are announcing to people that you are part of this group, and you are looking for approval because you belong to and are involved with this group.

These are the six benefits that people buy when they hire a consultant. Which apply to you and which of them are you trying to exploit? Are you exploiting the appropriate ones?

If you're not getting all the business that you want, or if you're not as successful as you'd like to be, then something is being done inappropriately. You may simply be focusing or targeting the wrong buying benefits.

When you're preparing your presentation materials, literature, and even yourself, make sure that you have analyzed and fully understand the primary buying motives of the client and state them clearly.

Chapter 2 Independent Contractor vs. Employee

With layoffs, downsizing, telecommuters, etc. sometimes it is difficult to identify an employee. Are they really employees or are they independent contractors? Does it really matter?

As an independent contractor, the payment that you receive is in gross dollars. The client doesn't take out any taxes. You become responsible for taxes, retirement, insurance, etc. Just because you say you're an independent contractor, doesn't make you an independent contractor.

Take this little test and see what side of the fence you are operating from.

☐ Yes ☐ No   Do you own you own business?

☐ Yes ☐ No   Do you have a business license?

☐ Yes ☐ No   Do you have an office?

☐ Yes ☐ No   Do you have assistants?

☐ Yes ☐ No   Do you have business signs (assuming your neighborhood allows it)?

☐ Yes ☐ No   Do you list your services in a business directory?

☐ Yes ☐ No   Do you advertise your services?

☐ Yes ☐ No   Do you have an IRS employer identification number?

☐ Yes ☐ No   Do you report employer payroll taxes and wages with the state?

☐ Yes ☐ No   Can you provide proof of liability insurance coverage?

☐ Yes ☐ No   Can you control the way the work is performed?

☐ Yes ☐ No   Can you set your own hours?

☐ Yes ☐ No   Is the duration of employment for a specific job?

☐ Yes ☐ No   Do you control where you work?

☐ Yes ☐ No   If you work on the client's premises, is it under that client's direction or supervision?

☐ Yes ☐ No   Do you determine the order and sequence that the work is perform?

☐ Yes ☐ No   Are you hired for the final result, and not asked for progress or interim reports unless it is a specific part of the contract?

☐ Yes ☐ No   Are you generally responsible for expenses?

☐ Yes ☐ No   Are you able to perform the services without the client's facilities (equipment, office furniture, machinery, etc.)?

☐ Yes ☐ No   Are you able to make a profit or a loss?

☐ Yes ☐ No   Do you hire and pay assistants?

☐ Yes ☐ No   Do you own office equipment or materials?

☐ Yes ☐ No   Do you have continuing liabilities?

☐ Yes ☐ No   Have you agreed to perform specific job for a price agreed upon in advance?

☐ Yes ☐ No   Are you responsible for the satisfactory completion of a job or are you legally obligated to compensate the client for failure to complete?

☐ Yes ☐ No   Are you restricted from taking other jobs at the same time you are doing work for the client?

☐ Yes ☐ No   Does the client's employees have duties similar to yours?

☐ Yes ☐ No   Does the client provide assistants to you?

☐ Yes ☐ No   As long you produce a result, which meets the contract specifications, can you be fired?

Now that you have answered the questions, let's look at how and why they are important in determining whether you are in independent contractor.

In the 1960s and 1970s, the Internal Revenue Service began to aggressively pursue employment tax audits. The audits sought to reclassify workers as employees instead of independent contractors for purposes of generating more taxes for the federal government.

Resistance from business forced Congress to place a temporary ban on such reclassification activities. In 1986, Congress modified the ban. As a result, in the 1990s, businesses were facing renewed employment tax audits on a comprehensive basis.

The determination of whether an individual who performs services for another is performing services in the capacity of an employee, as opposed to services in the capacity of an independent contractor, carries with it significant federal tax consequences.

The employer:

- Must withhold income taxes from the wages paid to employees.

- Must withhold FICA taxes from employees' wages.

- Is required to match the amount of withheld FICA taxes.

- Must pay FICA and FUTA taxes on wages paid to employees, subject to credits for unemployment tax payments made into a state unemployment fund.

As an independent contractor:

- Your payment is not subject to neither income nor Social Security taxes withholdings.

- The client is not required to pay its share of FICA taxes or to pay FUTA taxes.

- You will pay the full amount of your Social Security taxes in the form of self-employment taxes.

- You are generally not entitled to protection from discrimination under either the Civil Rights Act of 1964 or the Age Discrimination in Employment Act of 1986.

- You do not receive rights relating to compensation provided by the Fair Labor Standards Act.

- You are not entitled to certain rights under the Occupational Safety and Health Act of 1970.

Under the common-law test, a worker is an employee if the employer has a right to direct and control when, where, and how the worker performs the tasks. The employer need not exercise control: it is sufficient that the employer has the right to do so.

The Internal Revenue Service has adopted 20 common-law factors to determine whether the requisite control or right to control exists to establish an employer-employee relationship. The IRS has not given any indication as to the weight to be assigned each of the various factors; however, there is an emphasis on the general notion of control.

The 20 factors are the extent to which:

1. The employer instructs the worker on how to complete the task.

2. The employer trains the worker.

3. The worker is integrated into the employer's business.

4. The worker renders his or her services personally.

5. The worker may hire, fire, supervise, or pay assistance.

6. There is a continuing relationship.

7. There are set hours of work.

8. Full-time work is required.

9. The worker works on the employer's premises.

10. The employer sets the order or sequence of work completion.

11. The worker reports orally or in writing.

12. The worker is paid an hourly, weekly, or monthly salary.

13. The employer pays the worker's business and/or travel expenses.

14. The employer furnishes the worker's tools or materials.

15. The worker does not have a significant investment in the tools or machinery.

16. The worker has no potential to realize a significant profit or loss.

17. The worker may work for others simultaneously.

18. The worker may make services available to the general public.

19. The employer has the right to discharge the worker.

20. The worker has the right to terminate the relationship.

Since all of these factors may not be pertinent in any given situation, and since all of them may not support the same result, commentators describe the following seven factors as the most important:

- The degree of control exercised by the principal over the details of the work.

- Which party invests in the facilities used in the work.

- The opportunity of the worker for profit or loss.

- Whether the principal has a right to discharge the worker.

- Whether the work is part of the principal's regular business.

- The permanency of the relationship.

- The type of relationship that the principal and worker believe they are creating.

If you have any questions about whether or not you are an independent contractor or not, talk with your CPA or call the state. The state is interested in working with you to determine your status. They have a form (Determination of Employment Work Status for Purposes of State Employment Taxes and Personal Income Tax Withholding) which will help in the determination of whether your are operating as an independent contractor.

Most of these factors establishing you as an independent contractor are covered throughout the book. However, here are a couple of items for your consideration.

CITY BUSINESS LICENSE

If your business is going to operate within the law, it may be necessary to obtain a license or permit in the city or county in which your business will be conducted. If a service business performs any portion of its work in other cities outside of its operational center, additional license(s) may be required in those cities.

Home-based businesses are not permitted to change the appearance of the neighborhood. Home-based businesses may be prohibited from using advertising or equipment that can be viewed from the street. Some cities restrict all home-based business operation.

Business licenses provide the city with a source of revenue and a means of controlling the types of businesses that operate within their jurisdiction. Different types of businesses may be subject to special restrictions or zoning. Repair services may be allowed, but only if they do not involve the use of toxic chemicals. Food services may be disallowed, but the city may allow the home as an administrative office for the business.

City business licenses are renewable yearly (January-December) or annually. The cost of a city business license is around $100 per year.

FICTITIOUS NAME STATEMENT (FNS)—DOING BUSINESS AS (DBA)

Names that suggest the existence of additional owners must be registered as fictitious business names. This is also known as filing a DBA, "Doing Business As." The cost is between $50-$125.

The simplest way to accomplish the filing of a DBA is to contact the local newspaper. The newspaper has the forms and the knowledge of what needs to be done and how to do it. Fill out the paperwork and the newspaper processes the statement with the county clerk.

Another method is to call the county clerk. The clerk will mail the papers or go on-line for the form. Return the completed statement to the clerk, and the clerk files the statement. Newspapers will send flyers advertising their services. Within 30 days after filing a Fictitious Name Statement, a copy of the statement must be published in a newspaper of general circulation in the county in which the principal place of business is located. The notice must appear once a week for four successive weeks.

A fictitious name statement expires five years from the date it was filed.

INSURANCE

There are several types of insurance. However, as a small business, you may not necessarily need them all, all the time. Here is a quick break down of what type of insurance there is and when you may need it.

Most of us know about automobile insurance since we have it for our current vehicle. As a home-based business, you may want to have the business pay for the insurance. The insurance might be a business expense. Talk to your bookkeeper or accountant about the feasibility. Talk to your current agent and let them know that you are using your vehicle for business. Some of the basic questions include: are you going to be driving more than before, or are there going to be other people (non-family) driving the car. These factors may or may not affect your current rate.

Business property insurance, as the name suggests, is insurance for your business property. Businesses outside the house find this insurance useful and necessary. As a home-based business, a rider to your homeowner's or renter's insurance could be in the range of $50 per year for $5,000 worth of coverage.

As an individual, you probably have property insurance to cover those items that you currently own. As with auto insurance, check with your accountant to see if this expense can be paid by your business.

Computer insurance, in our opinion, is questionable for a home-based one-person business. Finding a company to insure your computer and hoping that they will be around when you file a claim is of utmost importance. Surfing the internet will provide several sources. Talk to friends and family in the computer business to find what they think is best. Check with your current homeowner's policy to find out what the coverage may be. Implement backups and procedures so that if the computer fails, you already have most of it handled.

As an individual, you probably already have health insurance. The business might be able to pay for this expense. If you have a spouse or children, you also might be able to provide coverage for them. Check with your accountant because in order to do this legally, there are some rules that you must follow, such as your wife and children must be working for you and receiving a payroll check. Also, if you are providing health insurance for yourself and have employees, you may have responsibilities to your employees and their health insurance.

Disability insurance is important for a one-person business because when you aren't working, you may not have any income coming in. However, disability insurance tends to be costly. Talk to your current insurance agent or find a company that specializes in disability insurance.

You may have watched television or listened to the news and heard about malpractice insurance, especially with doctors or lawyers. Malpractice insurance is insurance about incompetence. If the doctor, through incompetence, hurts you, then you would file a lawsuit and the doctor's malpractice insurance would administer the suit.

However, as a consultant, you may want to explore errors-and-omissions insurance. This insurance is not about your incompetence but instead covers things you forgot to tell the client that caused the client injury. Errors-and-Omissions insurance is becoming common when an individual is asked to be a board member of an organization. Then, if the organization is sued where the person is (or was on) the board, the individual is not sued separately as an individual. If you belong to a club, association or trade group, ask if the organization includes a membership benefit access to errors-and-omissions insurance.

If your one-person business is actually you and another person, consider partnership insurance. We would recommend that you explore partnership insurance in a business relationship with everyone except your spouse. The rules, regulations and laws governing marriage are extensive and if you want a divorce, there is a legal roadmap.

On the other hand, if you are a partner with a family member or a best friend, ending the relationship often gets uncomfortable and difficult. Also, as a partner, your partner might enter into contractual relationships that you don't know about, yet you are still liable. Partnership insurance would cover these type of problems.

Product liability is useful if you are making or creating a new product—you are manufacturing the product. Check with other companies that are producing a similar product and ask who covers their liability and contact that company. If you are using a product already produced, product liability is usually not needed or required.

General liability insurance is a catch all for *other*. Frequently if you are bidding on government or municipality contracts, they may require that you have a minimum dollar value of liability insurance. Ask the company requiring the insurance if they have sources that they have heard others use or go back to your insurance agent to inquire about coverage.

Workers Compensation is insurance to cover those people that work for you. As an owner of a business, you can choose whether you want workers compensation for yourself. It's your business and we believe that you would have your best interest in mind and therefore workers compensation is optional.

However, if you hire people, workers compensation provides benefits to employees who are injured or become ill during the course of or due to employment. State disability is for injuries or illnesses that are not work-related. These are handled by the Employment Development Department (EDD). State Disability Insurance (SDI) is automatically deducted from the employee's paycheck.

The long and short of insurance for your business is simply this: after you've established yourself as an independent contractor and as a real working business, you'll want to make sure that you've appropriately covered your assets though the appropriate level of insurance protection.

EMPLOYER IDENTIFICATION NUMBER (EIN)

As a one-person business, which is not incorporated, you want the business to be a business. You want to build credit in the business name and you want the business to be the name on record when it's the business doing the work. The EIN helps to establish that identity.

The form (IRS SS-4) is very easy to fill out and can be found on-line. The questions range from name, address and phone number to type of entity (sole proprietor, partnership, etc.), date business started, principal activity, etc.

Talk to your accountant about EIN so that the information they fill out and file is correct. If you have any questions about an EIN, your accountant typically has the answers.

Chapter 3 Tips for Successfully Selling Services

No matter what you're offering in consulting services, there are certain universal axioms that guide the selling and buying processes. Understanding what they are, how they work, and how to apply them will increase your sales.

In order to be successful in any sales effort, the offering must be appropriate. Appropriate is defined as being correct and proper. Is what you're offering correct and proper (appropriate) for the market you're targeting, for the geographic area where you're located, for the group that you're addressing, and for the prices involved?

It's not about right or wrong, or good and bad. It's simply about appropriate. Teaching people to snow ski is an excellent service, but not in Palm Springs, California. This doesn't make skiing lessons a bad service nor does it make Palm Springs a bad marketing region. The service is inappropriate for the market, or the market is an inappropriate place to be offering the service, whichever perspective or viewpoint you choose to take.

Examine the services, markets, advertising methods, and sales methods and most importantly, the budgets. Make sure that everything is appropriate before you make the commitment to go ahead.

MONEY BACK GUARANTEES

Here's one of the ground rules for success in the service business:

Offer a 100 percent, no hassle, unconditional, money back guarantee.

1. You're guaranteeing your services because if you don't perform, you probably won't get paid.

2. People see what they believe, and obviously this must be a quality service because you wouldn't give that kind of a guarantee on poor service.

3. The response rate for people actually asking for a refund is so low that unless you're not performing at all, they're probably not going to ask for the refund.

Here's a guarantee that you see everyday but have probably never used. Look on the side of a box of breakfast food. *If for any reason you're unsatisfied with this product, write us for a full refund of the purchase price.* Can you see yourself asking for a full refund for a half-eaten box of breakfast food? The offer is genuine. They'll send you the money back, but who wants to go through the hassle?

Some people say, "I can't offer that kind of a guarantee; I'll go broke because I cannot guarantee success." Remember that what is guaranteed is the work that is done, by you—not the results.

When contracting with a client to perform services, you must define what the client believes constitutes complete services and agree to them in writing. Once it has been agreed how the work is to be done, then complete the contracted work and live up to the commitments that were made.

You have no control over whether the client uses the information properly, uses the information at all, or has any success in using it. That is out of your control.

FREE OR FEE

One of the most common questions asked is: Should the first meeting with a potential client be free or fee?

The most powerful form of convincing a client to purchase is called sample selling. Few of us would purchase a vehicle without a test drive or a sampling of the features and performance. One of the best techniques for getting prospects to come and see us is to offer the first session for free. This gets the parties interested.

Offering to assist a prospect on a no-charge basis is an excellent way to introduce your skills and services to the prospects. Unfortunately, as consultants, once you give away some of your services, many people begin to believe that the services are worth what they pay for them—nothing.

Rather than opening yourself up to a flood of no profit consultations, ask for a nominal donation (for example $20) for a favorite charity.

This simple device benefits everyone because:

1. You get the prospect to pay you a visit so you can explore the possibility of working together.

2. By requesting a tax-deductible donation, you stop people who aren't serious from coming and wasting your time.

3. The charity benefits each time a visit is made.

Regardless of what arrangements you make with a client, it is in your best interest to spend about ten minutes of the first meeting obtaining the answers to these five questions:

1. What are your goals and objectives?

   Don't guess at the prospect's needs no matter how astute you are. Let the prospect tell you what they're looking for. Later on, you can add your assessment of their needs to the conversation or proposal.

2. What are the impediments to your achieving these goals?

   Let the prospect tell you what they think needs to be done to correct the deficiencies. Even if it's incorrect, it'll give them a greater feeling of importance if they believe that they've got the problems figured out and are hiring a consultant because it's easier than doing it themselves.

3. How do you feel about change?

   Consultants have been known to cause more change per hour than any employee. If a prospect has an attitude of fix it but don't change it, you can be assured that consulting services are being considered as an excuse for internal problems that they feel cannot be corrected and all they want is someone to blame (remember the chainsaw consulting on page 2).

4. If you could have three wishes granted for the success of your organization, what would they be?

   Let the prospect tell you what their goals and ambitions are. Once you know what they expect to accomplish, it becomes much easier for you to develop a proposal that fits their defined needs rather than your assessment of their needs.

5. Have you ever used consultants before?

   If a prospect has never used consultants before, they may tend to treat you as an employee. If this is the case, you will have to educate them on how to correctly and effectively work with consultants. This is a question that you will have to assess because if you aren't interested in schooling these individuals, you may not want to have them as clients.

TIMING

A serious consideration when offering consulting services is the timing. For every service, there exists a window of opportunity where the prospect will perceive that your services are more valuable than at any other time. By locating this window of opportunity and making your services known, you'll have more business.

For example, right after an earthquake, earthquake consultants flourished. Several years after the earthquake you rarely hear about consultants that specialize in them.

Another good example is security consultants. Unfortunately, the perceived value for the service is usually after someone has been robbed. It is then that the victims realize that they need a burglar alarm system. The professional alarm companies recognized this window of opportunity and derive their sales leads from the police burglary and vandalism reports.

In both of these examples, the need has not changed, but the public's perception of that need has. The height of the public's perceived need is the window of opportunity that consultants look for.

What event, or series of events, will occur that will make the prospect believe that your services are more valuable at this particular time than any other?

FAMILIAR AND NON-THREATENING

We tend to do things based on the way we perceive the world around us. At different times in our lives, at different times in our careers, different things are more familiar than others. We respond best when what we're being offered is familiar and non-threatening.

Many things in the world are threatening to people. For example, language may become threatening, especially *techno-babble*. In fact, technical terms about a product may be threatening rather than reassuring. One of the primary concerns in today's world of technology is that technologists have a tendency to get overzealous about explaining the technology rather than the benefits.

You're not buying the product; you're buying the benefits. When asked, "How does that work," the best response is, "Very well; press the button and watch it." A technical dissertation may cause the prospect to be repulsed by the answer.

There's nothing wrong with explaining the technology, so long as it is familiar and comforting to the listener. If it's not, then what you have done is turn them away from you.

There are other things that cause people to feel uncomfortable. Clothing styles tend to make you either stand out or blend in. When you stand out, the chances of getting through to the prospect are reduced. John T. Molloy's books, *New Dress for Success* and *New Woman's Dress for Success*, were written based on research for what is appropriate in different industries and different parts of the country.

The best way to overcome this dress code situation is to make a telephone call to the prospect's office and find out what the dress code is. You'll find that when you fit in you make the prospect more comfortable.

You have to examine each situation on a case-by-case basis, and then say to yourself, "This is where I can make the prospect feel as comfortable as possible." Put them in familiar surroundings and be non-threatening. Determine which characteristics are familiar and non-threatening, and use them to your advantage.

CREDIBILITY

When you buy a product, you can see it, feel it, smell it, touch it, or taste it. When you offer services, the prospect prefers to experience us and to build trust and eliminate their doubts about hiring us. This is called *establishing credibility*.

The hierarchy for establishing your credibility as service providers is as follows:

1. Personal experience—when clients have first-hand experience with your skills they have the inherent knowledge of what your capabilities are and whether you are a fit for their needs.

2. Recommendation from a trusted peer—prospects have defined job responsibilities that parallel those of others. A solid recommendation from one of these peers who have experienced your skills is a great way to get an opportunity to offer your services.

3. Recommendations from a prospect's vendor—many prospects will ask for referrals from vendors that are doing good work for them and whose opinion they value.

4. Promotional materials generated by the consultant—you can put anything into your promotional materials that you think will attract and impress the prospect. Unfortunately, most prospects are skeptical of promotional materials and prefer some form of experience, either directly or by referral, as to your capability to handle their requirements.

Establishing your credibility with your prospect is an integral part of being hired because people see what they believe and when they believe that you are credible, they tend to trust and subsequently hire you.

FIND A NEED AND FILL IT

Regardless of your area of expertise, you have one or more prime markets where your skills are perceived as indispensable. Once you locate these markets, it becomes a matter of mechanics, rather than magic, to find the clients.

There are a variety of situations and conditions that actually determine who your prospect base is and how to get to them. These questions will show you step-by-step how to target your market and get contacts. Answer the questions as diligently as you can. You want to ask an associate to assist you with the process to keep you focused. After you've completed the task, set the answers aside for a day or two and then answer them again.

Most people find that by the time they've completed answering the last questions, the first ones have changed because they've thought more logically about the overall market they're targeting.

1. What is your area of expertise in terms of its title, content, appeal, and benefits?

    - Title of your service—the grabber that gets their attention.

    - Content—a sub-heading that describes in some detail what you're going to provide.

    - Benefits—WIIFT, what immediate usefulness does the service have?

2. Who would be most likely to benefit from this service? Does it apply primarily to an occupation, a hobby, legislation, etc.?

3. What leads you to believe that this industry or group is the best target market for your services? Explain. For example, will you use a survey, personal knowledge of industry, media, government legislation, or industry legislation? What have you read and where did you read it, which leads you to believe that you have a service that will sell?

4. Where would the most likely candidates look to find this information? Is the service or topic geared toward a specific physical locale, country, or culture, or does it lend itself to a particular type of organization?

5. How do you go about locating a list that service the needs of these individuals? Can you define and locate a directory or listing of the clubs,

organizations, or industries that fit into your definition of the perfect client? Where and how do you get this directory?

6. How do you go about making initial contact: mail, telephone, fax, personal visit, e-mail, web, or free presentation?

7. When is the best time to contact these organizations? Are there calendar considerations, yearly considerations, daily considerations, weekly considerations, or time of day considerations?

8. What materials and customization will be needed to close your deal—workbooks, handouts, A/V materials, or industry research?

9. How do you research the prospect's needs so you can tailor your materials—industry survey, specialist survey, company survey, legislative research, or industry research?

10. What is the best way to solicit and follow up with these prospects—mail, telephone, fax, e-mail, or personal visit?

11. What industry standards, words, or information will you need to include in your materials and presentation to convince the prospect that you are knowledgeable and credible?

12. What type of credentials or experience will you need to convince the group or organization that you are the best person to present this material—formal credentials, industry credentials, hands-on industry experience, personal referral, showcase, or demonstration?

Chapter 4 Establishing Your Value

Consultants are complete, stand-alone businesses and are subject to the three elements of cost that enter into any business. These are: labor rate, overhead, and profit. Added together, these make up what is known as the daily (or hourly) billing rate. Here's the equation: daily labor rate + overhead + profit = daily billing rate.

ESTABLISHING YOUR FEE

Services must be correctly and fairly priced, or you'll never be profitable. Below is a simplified method to help you profitably price your services.

DAILY LABOR RATE

The Daily Labor Rate is your worth as a labor commodity. To accurately define this worth, you can look up your labor classification by geographic locale in the Wage and Salary Almanac at the library's reference section or visit http://www.salary.com.

This is an example of how to calculate your worth as a labor commodity:

1. $75,000 per year (a nominal figure in today's labor market) (12 months or 260 days).

2. A consultant works approximately 64 percent (168 days) of the time for the same amount of money.

3. $75,000 √ 168 = $446 per day or $56 per hour.

4. Overhead is approximately 90 percent.

5. Profit is approximately 10 percent.

Calculating Daily Billing Rate

Daily Labor Rate		$446
Overhead	90 percent of daily labor rate	$401
Profit	10 percent of daily labor rate + 10 percent of overhead	$ 85
Daily Billing Rate		$932 per day or $117 per hour

OVERHEAD AND DIRECT EXPENSES

People who provide services generate two types of expenses.

1. Overhead is the cost of being in business, and includes general operating expenses plus all other expenses that are incurred, regardless of how many clients there are or how much business you are doing. Rent is an example of overhead.

2. Direct expenses are those incurred for a particular client or a particular client's project. They are called direct because the client is charged for expenses directly. For example, the cost to fly to a meeting for the client is billed to the client.

Overhead is calculated on an annual basis and is a simple equation. It is the estimated total annual expenses for the business divided by the estimated total annual revenues for the business.

The anticipated cost of running the business is $67,500 and the revenues generated to be $75,000.

Category of Expense	Monthly	Annual
Part-time secretary	$1,000	$12,000
Office rent	1,000	12,000
Telephone and postage	550	6,600
Automotive	300	3,600
Personnel benefits/employment taxes	600	7,200
Equipment and supplies	300	3,600
Marketing costs	1,000	12,000
Dues and subscriptions	100	1,200
Business licenses and taxes	75	900
Insurance	300	3,600
Accounting and legal	200	2,400
Miscellaneous	200	2,400
Total	$5,625	$67,500

The equation is then: $67,500 √ $75,000 = 90 percent

The overhead weighs heavily in the total cost to the client. Also, the client has their own overhead to contend with and the lower the overhead, the better off they are because this is money they are giving to someone else—they are neither keeping it, or using it to pay employees. Employees are overhead! Overhead is the primary financial reason why consultants are used instead of employees—there is a much lower overhead factor!

PROFIT

Profit is whatever is left after you have paid yourself (salary) and paid for the operating expenses of the business.

We have assigned a nominal 10 percent profit to the equation, but you can use any number that makes sense to you and your operation. Of all the elements, this is the one with the most flexibility because making a profit is not essential for the business to operate. It may be essential for future growth, but based on pure mathematics, it is not necessary for the project under consideration to be successful.

Don't ignore profit. You're entitled to make a profit just like anybody else, but it's the first place you start to cut and make concessions in a proposal without affecting the payoff and actual operating expenses.

When calculating profit, take the percentage from the sum of the overhead and the daily labor rate. The overhead is money that is NOT earning interest in the bank, so it's acceptable to make a profit on the money you're using to run the business to compensate for the interest you are not earning on it.

VALUE CONSIDERATIONS

Regardless of your financial calculations, many factors affect the actual fees that consultants charge. Some of the common factors are as follows:

1. Reputation affects the fee a consultant can command and may be based on how noted the consultant is in the field. The more distinguished, the more that can be charged. Fees are a function of value, and value is a function of reputation in the eyes of prospects.

2. Prevailing Rate is sometimes a daily or hourly standard rate dictated by tradition within a given field or in a given area of the country.

3. Value Added Fees are based on the results that the consultant expects to achieve and their worth to the client in real dollars. The consultant's track record and reputation play heavily in this approach.

Don't be afraid or ashamed to work at a reduced fee or at a prevailing rate. Many consultants who have inflexible policies about their rates go bankrupt waiting to be paid what they think they're worth. Dollars are dollars and if you make yours a nickel at a time, that's OK—they still pay the bills.

The simplest philosophy is this: "When your calendar is filled with full fee assignments, you cannot afford to work for a reduced fee. Until that day, don't turn down any assignment that pays you for your efforts."

CONTRACTS

To ensure that all parties in an arrangement understand everything that is involved, a written agreement is a necessity. These agreements are not intended for litigation purposes as much as they are for the purpose of clarification and understanding.

You MUST insist on working with a written contract. Aside from the obvious legal protection with a contract, it has many other advantages. One of the important advantages of a contract is that it demonstrates to the client that you take your own business responsibilities seriously and professionally.

Here's a special tip that has been gained through years of experience: If you quote a fee on a fixed-price or fixed-fee basis, quote an odd number. If your calculation shows that the total cost of doing the client's assignment is $10,511, resist the tendency to round the quotation to $10,500. Doing so gives the appearance that you rounded up, not down.

Several styles of contracts are included here as a foundation for your business and we encourage you to use them, in any form you find expedient, as often as possible to ensure that all the parties involved get what they want and need out of the consulting arrangement. Use these agreements as the basic form for your needs, and then take the completed filled-in form(s) to legal counsel. Counsel then can watch for specifics, which apply to the situation. Generally, it costs less to review a document than to create it.

The contracts and agreements most commonly used by consultants are:

- Letter of Agreement

- Formal Contract or Legalese Style

- Contingent Commitment Agreement

- Work-for-hire Agreement

The actual proposal that is prepared and submitted may be of different formats and lengths. Any agreement is only as valid as the integrity of the persons who are involved.

LETTER OF AGREEMENT

The Letter of Agreement can be informal or formal. With some clients, informal is better. Be sure to break down the essence and particulars of the agreement. This letter causes both of you to recall more clearly and behave more predictably.

Sample Letter of Agreement

February 30, 2025

John Smith
Power Drill Repair Service
1212 Central
Los Angeles, CA 98765

Dear John:

Thanks for the opportunity to be of service to you and your firm. As a long-time user of a power drill, I have an appreciation for the work that you do. We propose to do a combination of a direct mail and telemarketing campaign designed to resell your existing client base and garner new business as well.

What we propose to do is as follows:
- Supply you with database software, install it, and train your staff. The delivery and training will occur simultaneously with the rest of the program as described below. Cost: $850.
- Input names and address that you provide for a customer database. The database entry should take less than six weeks. Cost: 15¢ per entry.
- Develop four 8½"x11" advertising flyers. We'll create the basic piece, write the copy, and sketch out the layout. An outside house will do the actual typesetting. The first flyer can be ready within six weeks. The subsequent flyers are every 90 days. Cost: $4,000 for the set of four.

Our terms for this program are as follows:
- A deposit of $2,000 is to accompany a signed copy of this letter contract.
- All materials and labor will be itemized. When each of the tasks as outlined above is completed, we will invoice you for the amount due. The first $2,000 will be credited back to you, and the balance will be due and payable net seven days.
- All work, artwork, advertising copy, etc., will be submitted to you for your final approval.

If you have any questions or require any additional information, please feel free to call on us.

Sincerely
John Doe
John Doe

I agree with and approve the letter contract outlined above and want to proceed with the program as proposed.

_____   _____
John Smith   Date

FORMAL CONTRACT OR LEGALESE STYLE

Many people who have transitioned from large corporations and the military or aerospace industries prefer these because they include contingency provisions for just about anything that might go wrong. This is a more comprehensive type of agreement, which actually incorporates a consulting contract, statement of work, confidentiality agreement, terms, conditions, and timeline all in a single document.

The caution in using these lengthy and complicated agreements is that if you are not comfortable with them or do not understand the exact meaning of the terminology used, seek the assistance of someone who does.

These contracts are not intended as an instrument to cheat you but if you inadvertently sign and agree to something that you do not understand, you may be committing yourself to performance that is either not what you intended, or that is outside your scope of capability to provide.

Sample Formal Contract

THIS IS A CONTRACT BETWEEN:

John Doe
123 Main St
Los Angeles CA 98765
(213) 555-9502
and
Byte Size Computer School
11460 Warm St
Central Valley, CA 92777
(800) 529-2093

SERVICES: John Doe will perform the services to develop a planning document and report, which includes recommended businesses and seminars to be offered to these businesses that will enable Byte Size Computer School (Byte Size) to offer a professional series of seminars and workshops to businesses in its Radius of Influence (ROI).

TASK 1: Develop and establish a ROI for Byte Size that reflects the most likely business population for the courses to be offered.

TASK 2: Perform research to determine the business profiles and demographics that reflects the most likely business population for the courses to be offered.

TASK 3: Develop a telemarketing survey, including forms and scripts, for use by Byte Size that will accurately reflect the wants and needs of the targeted business community for the Byte Size courses.

COMPENSATION: As full compensation for the services to be performed by John Doe, Byte Size shall pay John Doe per the terms and agreement as outlined below:

- The sum of $1,000 shall be paid to John Doe at the onset of work, which is to be coincidental with the signing of this agreement.

- The sum of $2,000 shall be paid to John Doe upon completion of the three (3) tasks as outlined above.

In support of this effort, it is mutually understood, and agreed to by both John Doe and Byte Size, that Byte Size will supply to John Doe full and complete description of all goods, services, contracts, and/or related items that are to be included and/or incorporated into the services as proposed. If requested and required, at the completion of the project, John Doe shall surrender any and all documents and/or articles loaned to him by Byte Size in support of this project.

DELIVERY OF ITEMS/COMPLETION OF TASKS: All task items, #1 through #3, as delineated herein, shall, to the greatest extent practicable, be completed and accomplished to the satisfaction of Byte Size within 90 calendar days of the signing and acceptance of this agreement.

TRAVEL EXPENSES: Reasonable, out-of-pocket travel expenses (tourist-class transportation, hotel, and meals) incurred by John Doe in connection with any trip made by John Doe at the request and with prior approval of Byte Size will be paid by Byte Size.

INCIDENTAL EXPENSES: All mutually agreed upon expenses, which are either initialed or agreed upon in writing, actually incurred by John Doe, incidental to the services performed, will be paid by Byte Size.

INVOICE AND PAYMENT: John Doe shall submit invoices for services and expenses incurred (including receipts for items in excess of $25) and Byte Size shall make payment within seven days of the date of the invoice.

CONFIDENTIAL INFORMATION: John Doe agrees not to disclose or to induce Byte Size to use any confidential information that may be acquired from any third-party during the term of this agreement. John Doe represents that he is free to disclose to Byte Size, without breach of any obligation to a third-party, any and all information needed to perform services under this agreement. John Doe further agrees to indemnify and hold Byte Size harmless from and against all losses, liabilities, damages, expenses, or claims against Byte Size based on a breach of obligation by John Doe to a third-party in disclosing any third-party property to Byte Size during performance of the services under this agreement. During the course of performing services, John Doe may become aware of and receive confidential information, including data, designs, ideas, methods, reports, plans, or other proprietary matters of Byte Size. John Doe agrees to receive and hold in strict confidence for and on behalf of Byte Size all information that John Doe creates in connection with or as a result of performing services under this agreement, including data, designs, ideas, methods, reports, suggestions, or other confidential information. John Doe agrees not to use, or disclose, any of such information to any person either during or after the termination of this agreement unless such information is, or becomes, public knowledge.

INTELLECTUAL PROPERTY: All inventions, innovations, discoveries, improvements, ideas, and suggestions (rights), whether patentable or unpatentable, conceived, made, reduced to practice, or created by John Doe, resulting from or arising out of the services performed by John Doe under this agreement and relating in whole or in part to the business of Byte Size, will be promptly communicated in writing by John Doe to Byte Size and shall become the sole property of Byte Size. John Doe represents and warrants that John Doe has no obligation to any third-party that would be breached by the disclosure and assignment of rights to Byte Size.

INDEPENDENT CONTRACTOR: John Doe, with respect to the services performed under this agreement, is acting as an independent contractor, and not as an employee. Other persons, firms, or corporations during this agreement may employ John Doe. Any employees or other personnel engaged by John Doe shall be under the exclusive direction and control of John Doe. John Doe shall assume and discharge for his own account all costs, expenses, and charges necessary or incidental to the performance of services (e.g., mileage, telephone charges, fax charges, etc.).

TERM AND TERMINATION: This agreement is effective from the date first written below and shall terminate when the terms and conditions on the attached Statement of Work have been completed. This agreement may be terminated by Byte Size by giving three (3) days notice to John Doe, in the event of death, illness or injury that will permanently prevent the performance of service required under this agreement, or if for any reason John Doe fails to perform any services as delineated in this agreement, after request by Byte Size, for a period of four consecutive weeks. Either party may terminate this agreement on breach of any of the terms by the other party by giving three (3) days notice to the other party. In the event that John Doe is in breach, and Byte Size cancels the contract, any advance monies shall be returned to Byte Size. In the event that Byte Size is in breach, and John Doe cancels the contract, any and all monies paid to John Doe shall remain the property of John Doe and shall not be required to be returned. Termination of this agreement for any reason shall not affect John Doe's obligation under paragraphs regarding Confidential Information and Intellectual Property and date is the date of receipt, since such date cannot be easily proved by the sender.

ENTIRE AGREEMENT: This agreement constitutes the entire agreement between the parties relating to the subject matter contained in it and supersedes all prior and contemporaneous representations, agreements, or understandings between the parties. No amendment or supplement of this agreement shall be binding unless executed in writing by the parties. No waiver of any one provision of this agreement shall constitute waiver of any other provision, nor shall any one waiver constitute a continuing waiver. In the event suit is brought to enforce or interpret any part of this agreement, the prevailing party shall be entitled to recover as an element of his costs of the suit, and not as damages, a reasonable attorney's fee to be fixed by the court. The "prevailing party" shall be the party who is entitled to recover the costs of suit, whether or not the suit proceeds to final judgment. A party not entitled to recover his costs shall not recover attorney's fees. No sum for attorney's fees shall be counted in calculating the amount of a judgment for purposes of determining whether a party is entitled to recover his costs or attorney's fees.

No waiver shall be binding unless executed in writing by the party against whom the waiver is asserted.

The terms, conditions, and statements contained herein are hereby mutually agreed upon as being the full and complete tasks required for the successful completion of this contract.

IN WITNESS WHEREOF, the parties hereto have signed on the day and year hereinafter set forth.

<u>John Doe</u>   Date

<u>Byte Size Computer School</u>   Date

CONTINGENT COMMITMENT AGREEMENT

One of the areas of concern to consultants is when they find themselves in a situation where they have an original idea that has not yet been developed and under the current laws, have no formal protection, but still need to disclose their ideas to another party or organization for purposes of mutual benefit.

The solution to this dilemma comes in the form of a seldom publicized, but widely used document known as a Contingent Commitment Agreement whose name pretty much sums up what it's all about:

1. It's an agreement.

2. It involves commitments on the part of both parties.

3. There are contingencies involved on the part of both parties.

Contingent Commitment Agreements are used to establish a mutually agreed upon value and a potential payment for knowledge and information that will result in a certain level or standard of performance, prior to divulging the specific information regarding the precise method for obtaining the desired result.

To give you an example of how they came about, consider a business plan for a new start-up enterprise. Until the business is started, there are no funds to hire critical employees. Without the critical employees to make the company viable, venture capitalists will not fund the new start-up. This is the perfect example of the old adage: Which came first—the chicken or the egg?

Here's how the problem has been handled and where the basic tenants of the agreement came from. The individual or group creating the business plan for the new start-up would advertise and interview for the needed key employees. Once the individual was found, both parties would sign an agreement that stated the following:

• The person writing the plan would be allowed to insert the resume' and qualifications of the selected individual into the plan.

• If the plan was funded, the person writing the plan committed to hire the individual whose resume' was added to the plan.

- The person whose resume' was included with the plan committed to quitting their current job and joining the new start-up organization as soon as the funding was in place.

Consultants have a similar problem when they reach a point where in order to obtain support, financing, or some other form of mutual profitability, the consultant must disclose to the other party, certain pertinent details of the idea or concept which once divulged, could be exploited without the involvement of the consultant.

Since the concept is incomplete, the consultant is not in a position, for whatever the reason, to obtain proprietary protection under the current intellectual property laws.

For consultants, the basic tenants of the agreement reflect the following:

- The consultant has an idea or concept that he or she believes is of value to the other party.

- The consultant needs to disclose the information to the other party to obtain support.

- The consultant wants the other party to provide support if what they say is accurate and of interest to the other party.

- If the representations of the consultant are true, the other party agrees to become involved in whatever manner is agreed upon. If the representations are not true, are already known to the other party, or are not of interest to the other party, the other party is prohibited from exploiting the idea or innovation without the consultant.

In other words, the consultant agrees to tell the other party what the idea will accomplish but not the specifics of how it is accomplished until both parties sign the agreement.

As with the other contractual documents outlined above, the Contingent Commitment Agreement is a legal contractual document that can be used in a court of law to recover damages if the need arises.

The Contingent Commitment Agreement contains the following items:

AA: Date of the agreement (day, month and year, for example 21st of May, 2005).

BB: Person or organization that is offering to divulge the information.

CC: Person or organization that is agreeing to receive the information.

DD: A full description of the relative merits and/or benefits of the idea or innovation including any sub-points.

EE: A description of the mutually agreed upon compensation including any sub-points.

FF: A signature of an independent, disinterested, third-party who will attest, by signing the document, to the veracity of the statements contained in the document including the willingness of the parties involved to sign the document without coercion.

AA

This is an agreement between BB and CC, which outlines the basic guidelines for a Contingent Commitment Agreement. The purpose of this agreement is to allow BB to disclose an idea and/or product to CC for the purpose of review, discussion, and the possibility of a mutually beneficial business relationship.

The basic tenants of this agreement are as follows:

1.   BB represents to CC the following: DD

2.   CC agrees to the following:

    a.   That if the representations presented by BB are, in fact, truthful and are of interest to CC, that CC agrees to enter into an agreement with terms and conditions to be negotiated to the mutual satisfaction of both parties.

    b.   That in the event that mutually satisfactory licensing arrangements are not reached by BB and CC, that CC:

- Shall have no rights or obligations under this agreement.

- Agrees that all designs, ideas, and intellectual property disclosed during this relationship are, and shall remain, the proprietary and exclusive property of BB.

- Will not use, cause to be used, or disclose, in any manner whatsoever, these proprietary items, and

- That all physical items including, but not limited to, prototypes, drawings, descriptions, and/or any manner of documentation or design which could be used to transfer the design characteristics represented in this agreement, shall not be kept, copied or distributed but shall, instead, be presented to BB at no charge to BB for his sole and exclusive use.

    c.   If the information, products, or materials presented and discussed by BB and CC during this meeting, were known to CC prior to the disclosure referenced herein by BB, that CC shall be under no obligation to compensate BB and that CC's sole obligation shall be that of confidentiality of the information, products, or materials presented and discussed by BB and CC during this meeting or meetings with the exception of the following conditions:

- Information, which at the time of disclosure, had been previously published or a matter of public record.

- Information that is published after disclosure unless such publication is a breach of this agreement.

- Information, which, prior to disclosure to CC was already in its possession, as evidenced by written records kept in the ordinary course of business by or by proof of actual use by CC.

- Information which, subsequent to disclosure, is obtained by CC from a third person who is lawfully in possession of such information, and not in violation of any contractual, legal, or fiduciary obligation to BB with respect to such information and who does not require CC to refrain from disclosing or using such information.

In the event that CC violates any term or covenant contained herein, BB, at any time thereafter, may pursue legal action in both law and equity, including injunctive relief.

This agreement represents the entire understanding and agreement between the parties hereto and supersedes all prior agreements and understandings, either oral or written, between them, with respect to the subject matter hereof. Any modifications of this agreement must be in writing and signed by all the parties hereto.

BB Signature	Printed Name	Date

CC Signature	Printed Name	Date

FF Signature	Printed Name	Date

WORK-FOR-HIRE AGREEMENT

Work-for-hire Agreements are a combination of a contract for services along with a nondisclosure agreement all rolled into one. They are normally used when the interface between the consultant and another party goes past the discussion stage and requires some form of actual work be accomplished on a subcontract basis.

They are used to mutually agree that when a subcontractor performs work for you (then you are the contractor) or when you are the subcontractor to a client, on what is considered proprietary development, and which may produce derivative works or products that might be of interest to the prime contractor or client, that:

1.   All of the work, including derivative work or new ideas that are created as a result of working on the idea belong to the prime contractor and not the subcontractor,

2.   That the prime contractor has the exclusive rights to all of the work, ideas, and/or innovations.

Because of recent rulings in the software industry, Work-for-hire Agreements have become an essential part of a consultant's process for assuring the rights to development efforts are not given away.

The courts have ruled that without a written Work-for-hire Agreement that any subcontracted work could come under ownership dispute and that the prime contractor could unknowingly be hiring a partner for all future exploitation of his or her ideas.

Work-for-hire Agreements spell out, in as much pertinent detail as necessary, the terms of the employment or subcontract agreement and what rights, if any, the employee or subcontractor would have to new works that were derived from the original work that was contracted for.

Pertinent information in Work-for-hire Agreements should include:

AA: The name of employee or independent contractor.

BB: The name of the person (consultant) or organization that is hiring the independent contractor.

CC: The date the work is to be completed.

DD: The state in which contract is executed.

Three detailed attachments:

Attachment A: Payment Schedule. In this attachment, you must describe, in exact detail, when AA will be paid and in what manner payment will be made. You must also define what will constitute a mutually agreed upon milestone or task that will signify that a particular payment is due and payable.

Attachment B: Duties. Here you must illustrate what AA has to produce, in order to get paid, by describing the work in detail. Besides the actual work, what AA may be expected to deliver such as detailed specifications, documentation, and so forth? In this attachment, you list what your responsibilities, as the client, will be in addition to payment of AA's invoice. These include providing hardware, technical specifications, workspace, or other mutually agreed upon components that will be required for AA to complete the task as defined.

Attachment C: Work Schedule. Here you must describe, in task-by-task detail, the payment of the monies described in Attachment A and the work described in Attachment B, in a time-oriented task outline. These tasks should include the delivery of and payment for all of the data, documentation, drawings, tooling, and other support elements that are considered to be a part of the overall project that the client is paying for.

INTRODUCTION: This is a Work-for-hire Agreement in which AA, an independent contractor, agrees to provide services to BB. BB shall pay AA according to the payment schedule set forth in Attachment A of this agreement, which is incorporated by reference herein.

DUTIES: AA agrees to provide the services for BB as per the specifications set forth in Attachment B to this agreement, which is incorporated by reference herein. BB shall supply AA all items listed in Attachment B prior to CC.

OWNERSHIP: In consideration for payment as set forth in Attachment A of this agreement, AA hereby assigns all rights in the work performed under this agreement to BB, including the right to apply for any and all appropriate patents, trademarks, trade secrets and/or copyrights that may result as a consequence of the work performed in BB's name.

AA understands that the work contracted for and described herein is a Work-for-hire, which shall be the exclusive property of BB.

Consistent with AA's recognition of BB's complete ownership rights in the work described in Attachment B, AA agrees not to use the work created under this agreement for the benefit of any party other than BB.

COMPLETION DATE: AA agrees to complete all work as per the schedule set forth in Attachment C of this agreement, which is hereby incorporated by reference herein.

TRADE SECRETS: All types of information relating to the work described herein and contracted for, including this agreement and its attachments, are to be considered the trade secrets of BB.

AA shall keep all trade secrets of BB confidential, and shall sign nondisclosure agreements when requested by BB.

ARBITRATION: Any dispute relating to the interpretation or performance of this agreement shall be resolved at the request of either party through binding arbitration. Arbitration shall be conducted in the state of DD in accordance with the then existing rules of the American Arbitration Association. Judgment upon any award by the arbitrators may be entered by the state or federal court having jurisdiction. The parties intend that this agreement to arbitrate be irrevocable.

GENERAL PROVISIONS

- AA may neither subcontract nor hire persons to aid in the contracted work without the prior written consent of BB.

- Any modifications to this agreement must be in writing and signed by both parties.

AA Signature   Date

BB Signature   Date

Attachment A: Payment Schedule

AA shall be paid in the following manner:

Attachment B: Duties

AA will be responsible for:

DD will be responsible for:

Attachment C: Work Schedule

AA agrees to complete the work described in Attachment B according to the following schedule:

Speaking Fee Schedule

Half-Day [up to 3 hours] $X,000

Full Day [up to 6 hours] $Z,000

DEPOSITS AND CANCELLATION POLICY
The deposit is 50 percent of fee and is required upon confirmation of booking. In the event of program cancellation, we will re-book on a mutually convenient date. If program is canceled by the client and not rescheduled, the deposit will be full and complete settlement.

TRAVEL EXPENSES AND ACCOMMODATIONS
All fees are as quoted, plus travel expenses. Rounds, Miller and Associates will book full coach airfare. Travel and expenses will be billed directly to the client if possible other wise they will be invoiced after the program has been completed. Accommodations will be billed directly to your organization.

SUPPORT MATERIAL
Materials for participants will be quoted, supplied, and invoiced as quoted.

AUDIO AND VIDEO RECORDING
Any nonprofit distribution of the program within your organization is permitted. A master copy of any recording will be supplied to and approved by Rounds, Miller and Associates. All other recordings and rights of reproduction and/or distribution must be cleared, in writing, with the speaker prior to the engagement.

BOOKS AND TAPES
Educational support materials can be made available if there is a written agreement to do so with the speaker.

CONTACT
Rounds, Miller and Associates
6318 Ridgepath Court
Rancho Palos Verdes CA 90275-3248
310-544-9502
310-544-3017 fax

OUR GUARANTEE
We guarantee that the performance of the speaker will meet or exceed both your standards and your expectations or your money will be refunded

Effective date: January 1, 2004

Chapter 5 Techniques for Promoting Services

Once upon a time, consultants simply hung out a sign and used word of mouth to get clients. Because of increased competition, vastly expanded markets, rapidity of information dissemination, population growth, and the perception that services are as valuable as goods, you no longer have the option of only using word of mouth advertising if you want to be profitable.

Marketing efforts for consultants divide into two generic categories: proactive and reactive. Historically, consultants have opted for the reactive methods, usually with disastrous results. On the other hand, those consultants who utilize the proactive methods generally have a backlog of business, clients and work when others can't seem to find any.

Many successful consultants use a combination of the two methods to help ensure an ongoing presence in the marketplace while actively promoting their services on a regular basis to a fresh audience.

Selling consulting services is no more difficult than selling products, but because consultants hardly had to sell themselves before, the process appears tedious. There is still reluctance on the part of consultants to get out there and scramble for the business. You perform services, and you tend to take the rejection of your services as a rejection of you.

In the world of proactive methods, it turns out that speaking, information products, and organizational involvement have the greatest return on investment.

The methods, tips, and techniques that follow are designed to assist all types of consultants to market their services. All of the information is practical, time-tested and field-proven methods. Nothing is theory. Everything described here works—but not all the time.

As with all marketing efforts, selling consulting services is a numbers game—the greater the number of prospects we educate to our skills and capabilities, the greater the number of leads and clients we'll obtain.

SPEAKING

There are numerous ways to promote your business with speaking. Chapters 6-9 go into detail on how to do so but here are a few.

Radio Talk Shows

With remote interview capabilities, the radio talk show circuit has become a viable marketplace for consultants. There are currently over 1,000 radio stations in the United States that feature a talk show format, with experts being interviewed by telephone.

The interesting part about being a guest on radio talk shows is that it not only gives you the opportunity to talk about and promote your own skills and talents, it also gives you a venue to sell tapes, books, and other information-based products.

A good press release, tied to current events, will also go a long way towards getting you booked on radio talk shows since they are looking for guests to speak about something that's of current interest to their listeners.

The following press release was successfully used to book Mike on radio talks shows nationwide.

Sample Press Release for Radio Talk Shows

For Immediate Release   FOR FURTHER INFORMATION CONTACT:
                                          Mike Rounds (800) 757-7671

"America's Work Force Goes Home—and Doesn't Come Back"

OVER 64 PERCENT OF ALL NEW BUSINESS START-UPS ARE HOME-BASED AND
THE NUMBER IS INCREASING BY 4 PERCENT PER YEAR!

"Americans have discovered that working for themselves, at home, is as lucrative and secure a position as a corporate job," states Mike Rounds, a specialist in marketing services, author, and instructor to thousands of entrepreneurs. "We've returned to the concept that made America strong—entrepreneurism!"

"The United States has become a service oriented country," states Rounds. "We don't manufacture the volume of products we once did—that's been sent offshore. But, we're still the largest consumer of goods and services in the world, and supporting these business functions doesn't require huge facilities and thousands of laborers to be successful—just paper, records, ingenuity, computer skills, and a second bedroom."

"Any services where you're paid for performance as opposed to presence are perfect candidates for conversion to a home-based business," states Rounds. "Transcription and accounting services are great examples. Cell phones, internet access and computers are the driving forces behind this revolution. There's no reason why the individual doing the work has to be physically located at the same facility with the person assigning the work.

Telephone communications let's people share the details and the material is simply transferred via the internet and physically printed wherever it's needed."

The economic advantages are obvious when you calculate the time and money savings involved with commuting, workspace, employer contributions and employee benefit packages. This makes the home-based worker highly competitive with employees and affords them the freedom of selecting both the hours they choose to work as well as how many of them they choose to work. "You're back to paying people proportionally for the quality and volume of work they actually do—not the seniority or status they've achieved with an organization."

According to Rounds, the four steps to successfully profiting from working from home are:
1. Review your skills and see what you could do from home—for money.
2. Research your market to see who's using those skills and what they're paying for them.
3. Set up your home-based service business.
4. Solicit as many prospects as you can find.

Mike Rounds, author of ***Marketing the One-Person Business***, offers a FREE report to anyone interested in promoting his or her business. He's been an independent contractor for over 20 years and helps individuals make the successful transition from employee to entrepreneur.

#

Mike Rounds is a professional speaker who shares his bottom line wisdom and advice with thousands of listeners each year. To interview him, call 800-757-7671.

You'll find the complete listing of the Radio Talk Show Directory listed by going to http://www.aim.org/join_us/radio_talk_show_directory.pdf.

This site claims to be—and in our opinion is—the most comprehensive radio station search engine on the internet. With links to over 10,000 radio station web pages and over 2500 audio streams from radio stations in the U.S. and around the world, listings show call signs, distance from selected cities and towns, frequency, format, and signal strength. http://www.radio-locator.com/.

If you prefer the paper version, you can order it from Accuracy in Media, Inc., 4455 Connecticut Avenue NW #330 Washington, DC 20008 202-364-4401 fax: 202-364-4098.

You can obtain step-by-step information of the process for booking yourself on these shows from the videotape *Talk, Talk, Talk* or a lists of radio talk shows, from http://www.RoundsMiller.com or by calling 310-544-9502.

A free web-based quiz creation, management, and reporting program radio station locator is compiled by Larry James mailto:LarryJames@AuthorsandSpeakersNetwork.com.

TELE-SEMINARS

For the best information about this topic, we're going to refer you to Dan Janal at 952-380-1554 (http://www.GreatTeleseminars.com) because he's become the acknowledged leader in this technology.

Tele-seminars are essentially a conference call that is monitored and controlled by you. You can either be the host interviewing the expert or the host/expert and giving the lecture. You're conducting a virtual seminar where people pay to not only listen in, but also have the ability to ask questions.

During the program, you, as the host, have an audio recorder running and create an audio recording of the program, complete with commentaries, questions, and answers. Then you can offer it for sale to both the people who paid to participate live (usually at a discount) or to others who are interested in the material but who couldn't get in on the live presentation.

The procedure for setting up a program is fairly easy and we're serious about contacting Dan. He has materials that will give you all the specifics you'll need to set up and conduct your own tele-seminars. His material also explains the inexpensive ways to reproduce, package, and distribute the material.

If you're an average host, you'll be able to create a new tape each month. If you're real creative, you can host a tele-seminar (or web-inar) every two weeks and have over twenty audio products per year. You'll be able to package them up as a series or set.

INTERNET AND WEB-BASED MATERIALS

The internet really is a great place to deliver volumes of material for very little money. Its principle function is as a high-speed information delivery vehicle that reaches most of the world at the speed of light. Since you're in the information business, it's a natural vehicle for supplying your clients with reinforcement material that they both need and are willing to pay for.

There are a variety of software programs and firms who can set up your speeches, training sessions, and support material to be offered on-line, in both a lecture format and an interactive participant venue.

Many consultants are using the web to deliver short video demonstration clips of their speaking and training skills. For example http://www.Clutterology.com has demo clips from Nancy's seminars. These are a fast way to give a prospect a demonstration of your skills without having to wait for your video demo tape to arrive in the mail.

You can also create video training clips using the Windows Media Recorder (http://www.microsoft.com) and deliver them, on-line, when the client needs them.

A great example of commercializing the entire process is Education To Go (http://www.ed2go.com) who currently offers their entire catalog of programs at over 750 colleges, universities, and adult schools, as a text only, semi-passive course. (Sort of like an on-line correspondence course.)

Several other firms like Webex (http://www.webex.com) can create courses with graphics, multimedia, and interactivity if your material requires those elements to be effective. Since this is fast paced technology, check out what's currently the hot technology before you start to convert you material.

Then, there's the sweat equity method where you create your own course using PowerPoint, or other multimedia presentation programs that allow the web site visitor to control the presentation material like an automatic slide show program. Whatever software delivery system you choose, you'll be making time, money, and technology tradeoffs regarding the effective delivery of text, graphics, audio, video, and software.

INFORMATION PRODUCTS

What do information products have to do with marketing your services? Plenty, because they serve the multiple purpose of positioning you as an expert in your field, provide credible marketing materials, and serve as a revenue generation system that can double or triple your income!

Fundamentally, there have always been logical reasons for consultants to create information and support products. The motivation behind this concept is exemplified in the old adage: publish or perish!

You'll probably recognize the cliché as coming from the world of academia because professors need to publish if they want to become tenured and promoted in the hierarchy of education. Consultants have the same concerns because we both deal in the same commodity—intellectual information.

The bottom line is that sending your book, tape, or other material to a prospect positions you as an expert and provides greater credibility on the topic than a person who doesn't have published materials.

There's another very important reason to publish and that's SWIS money (Sells While I Sleep). Consultants are information providers or service providers and when you're not providing services, you're not making money. The answer to this dilemma is to provide information products that generate revenues when you're not on the platform and even while you're sleeping.

Once you get past the advertising and promotional value of your products, you'll find that they allow you flexibility in setting your fees and alternate ways to generate revenues both at your presentations as BORS (Back Of Room Sales) and as SWIS money. For example, here are some typical production prices:

- 2 C-60 audiotapes with labels, 2-tape audio capsule with cover insert and amortized setup cost = $3.30; suggested retail price $29.95 (9:1 profit margin).

- Videotapes including a 6-hour videotape, case, cover sheet, and label are approximately $2; suggested retail price $39.95 (20:1 profit margin).

- A 96 page book, 8½"x11" including cover layout and printing costs (1,500 quantities) = $2.26; suggested retail price $19.95 (8½:1 profit margin).

- Tips Booklet: printing costs .55; suggested retail price $5 (10:1 profit margin).

AUDIOTAPES AND CD'S

First, we need to clear up a misconception about audiotapes vs. audio CD's—audiotapes are NOT going away. According to the latest statistics, the average U.S. household has 3.5 cassette players. If you want to record your information on audiotape, there will be a market out there.

On the other hand, if you decide to use the CD format, do some research to make sure your target market is predominantly CD based or you'll have a lot of high tech coasters on your product inventory shelves.

Second to books, audio is the best information product you can generate because it's a non-intrusive medium. If you think about it, even though books are highly revered and respected, they require that the reader dedicate time to read. Video material requires that you dedicate time, and unique equipment. Audio can be multi-tasked while working, driving, or jogging.

What you record on audio is pretty much up to you but the best material doesn't need a visual component. That means that if the audio has to be accompanied by pictures, a workbook, or effort other than listening, it's not quite as effective as something that stands alone naturally.

The most common audio products are live recordings. Digital recorders are under $200 and small enough to fit into your pocket or clip on your belt. With a digital master, you can create any other medium you want including CD's and high quality audiotapes.

Another technique requires a little more equipment and an interviewer, but it's fun and highly saleable. Its basic format is an interview style but it's different because you write down 100+ questions about your topic. This style is good if your audience follows you to the rest room to ask you questions after the program is over or if you are a trainer and have more material than the program allows time for.

When it's done, you'll have 101 of the most commonly asked questions about the topic as answered by you, one of the country's leading authorities.

If you're going to record, consider getting an inexpensive recording and editing software package. Accoustica (http://www.acoustica.com) sells a $25 package for Windows that will record, edit, import, and convert just about any audio to a CD format. It also allows you to stick a microphone into your computer and record it directly. Since it's an editor, you'll be recording, editing, and processing perfect digital masters every time.

Another technique that seems to sell well is taking your recorded material, dividing it into 12-18 modules, and recording it as a training set. Look at Tony Robbins or Stephen Covey—that's what they've done. Current statistics say that the average commuter spends about 20 minutes on a commute, so 20 minute cassettes or CD's are the most expeditious length.

Breaking up material into short sound bytes, whether it's practicing telephone techniques or psyching yourself up to be a better person, will keep the listeners' attention longer. The media has proven that sound bytes work best so if you were doing this kind of project, stay with the short tape concept and make the product conform to what the public says it wants.

You can get any kind of AV packaging you need at inexpensive prices from Rick Knight, Audio/Video Distributing Inc., 2045 S Valentia St Ste 13, Denver CO 80231, 800-538-6409, 303-751-6400 or 303-751-5880 fax.

VIDEOTAPES, VCDS AND DVDS

OK, now that we've got all the techies slobbering and drooling because we're now looking at the latest in technology, you need to look at the available technologies first before you get to the subject matter.

The big deal is DVD but let's get real, videotape is going to be around for a while and you can pretty much guarantee that virtually everyone in your audience has a VCR. After all, they're available at K-Mart (http://www.bluelight.com) for $39.95.

If you want to be your own video producer, director, and distributor, handheld video camera systems are $249 (new), $99 (used), and blank VHS tape is available at 99¢ for a 6-hour cassette.

What's even more exciting is that computer technology is making it super cheap and really easy to convert tape to CD-ROM and DVD using your computer. You can get a CD-ROM burner for about $30, a DVD burner for $99, and software packages to convert and copy to the DVD format for $20.

The Studio digital editing software is available for $99 from Pinnacle Systems (http://www.pinnaclesys.com) that allows you to digitize, edit and create a variety of digital mediums including CD-ROMs and DVDs.

Microsoft has the Windows Media Recorder for FREE at http://www.microsoft.com. This amazing piece of software allows you to take your video files and convert them for play on everything from a 28.8 modem on a web site though direct play from a CD.

Now that your techno-lust has been satisfied, let's look at the actual material you're going to put on the medium. This is what makes up the value component that the audience is really buying, the thing they see.

- The place to start, just like with audio, is with a tape of your live speaking performance. If the audience loved you in person, they'll probably want to take you home so they can experience you over and over again.

- Training programs usually have a high visual content, so the use of video helps to reinforce that concept especially, if you're using graphs, charts, props, or other visual aids. If your audience needs pre-training to get them ready for your big day, you can pre-record the material that they need to know and understand before you arrive. Of course, videotaping the training session so the attendees can use it as reinforcement material is a natural.

- Another is the material that you won't have time to cover in the training session. Consider taping the extra hours of material that are needed but that the organization just can't spare the time to have you deliver in person.

- If the training requires ongoing or updated sessions, consider using video to stay in touch or to conduct training without having to jump on an airplane and show up in person.

- This one sounds strange but you might be surprised at how well it works. Gather 10-20 questions from the attendees, answer them on videotape, and send the client the tape together with permission to make as many copies as necessary. This is the next best thing to answering their questions from the platform plus it gives the added benefit of conducting a one-on-one session with the client.

BOOKS

Of all the information delivery vehicles you can create, a book still gives the most credibility and opens the most doors for profits.

We can speak from first-hand experience about the credibility of having published on a particular topic—both positive and negative. We've landed clients because of the materials we've published. We've lost speaking engagements to others consultants who weren't necessarily better or more knowledgeable, but who had published specifically on the topic that the meeting planner wanted.

You don't need to be published by a major New York publisher to be successful. Self-publishing is far more lucrative to the consultant than licensing the rights to your book or manual. According to information complied by Dan Poynter:

- There are 5 large publishers in New York,

- There are 300-400 medium-sized publishers,

- Most initial print runs are 5,000 copies,

- A larger publisher must sell 10,000 books to break even,

- A successful nonfiction book sells 7,5000 copies,

- 5.4 percent of books purchased are on the internet such as Amazon.com.

Here's an important point to consider when writing for money—the reader is primarily, if not exclusively, interested in themselves—not you! If you're writing to sell books and make money, make sure that the focus and benefits are for the reader. When you're rich and famous people will care about the way you vote and then you can write your memoirs and have a best seller.

In the meantime, consider writing how-to books that tell the reader, step-by-step how to accomplish what they want to achieve. You can weave your personal experiences and philosophies into the book, but make the focus reader centered.

Workbooks or how-to books are among the best selling types of books in the world. Following our concept of follow the money, it makes sense to produce this type of book to obtain maximum return on your investment. We have written several books. They are all how-to books, workbooks, manuals, or guidebooks—whichever term you prefer.

Here are some simple secrets for writing profitable books:

1. Write workbooks with scholars (2" wide) margins. These wide margins are great for taking notes or for adding your own special tips.

2. Use a 12-point serif (the ones with the little tails) font. Kids may be able to read little type but older adults can't.

3. Use a word processor like Word or WordPerfect. They're widely used, easy to learn, powerful, and provide all the elements you'll need to create a good looking finished book.

4. Design your books using 8½"x11" pages in 16-page signatures. Printers use a master sheet of paper that has 8 pages per side which when printed, is folded and trimmed to make a 16-page signature. You'll pay for the 16-pages whether you use it or not so write in 16-page increments. To make the book appear substantial plan on about six signatures or 96 pages.

5. Get an ISBN (International Standard Book Number) so you can individually identify all of your products (not just books). The ISBN is a unique machine-readable identification number. Amazon.com and Barnes and Noble will insist you have an ISBN so you might as well do it right away. Obtain the ISBN from R.R. Bowker at 800-537-7930 or http://www.Bowker.com or http://www.ISBN.org ($300 for 10 numbers). After you get your ISBN, put it on all your books and other products along with a UPC bar code so you can offer the material for retail sales. You can get software from AccuGraphix (http://www.bar-code.com) (800-872-9977) to add it into your back cover design or have your cover designer do it for you.

6. Library of Congress Control Number (LCCN), which appears on the copyright page, enables subscribers (like libraries) to the Library of Congress catalog card service to order cards by number. To get complete information on obtaining a Library of Congress number for your publication visit their web site (http://www.loc.gov/faq/catfaq.html).

7. If you're going to offer your book at retail, consider having a four-color cover designed. If you're selling your book via mail order or as a workbook for your programs, use a two-color cover for cost savings. You can have covers designed, complete with camera-ready artwork, for $150-$660 depending on colors and complexity by The Printing Press in Carson, California (contact Leslie Sears at 310-538-3321) or by Karen Ross (http://www.kgross.com) 310-397-3408, she did the cover for this book.

8. The best printing prices available for books and workbooks are from Short Run Solutions. You can print a 112-page workbook, 8½"x11", for $1.64 workbook in a 2,000 piece quantity. Contact Reg Frechette at 310-640-

0668. Here are typical soft cover book and workbook printing prices which includes setup and 2 color cover:

Quantity	96 Pages	112 Pages	128 Pages	144 Pages
500	$3.17/book	$3.45/book	$3.73/book	$4.01/book
1000	$2.69/book	$2.85/book	$3.00/book	$3.16/book
1500	$1.96/book	$2.09/book	$2.21/book	$2.33/book
2000	$1.54/book	$1.64/book	$1.75/book	$1.86/book
2500	$1.33/book	$1.43/book	$1.53/book	$1.62/book

9. Keep ALL graphics and clip art to 300 DPI. If you need higher resolution and detail, the cost will go up rapidly.

10. Make the cover price $20 or multiples of $20. This is ATM money and in a seminar where there is some confusion and rapid purchasing of product, $20 bills are very easy to handle and don't require making change.

11. Contact Para Publishing, Dan Poynter, PO Box 8206-890, Santa Barbara CA 93118-8206, (http://www.parapublishing.com) 805-968-1379 to purchase the bible of the industry, The Self-Publishing Manual $19.95 plus shipping.

BOOKLETS

Based on results, the best credibility enhancer is a book, but if you want to create a more definitive focus or expand your area of expertise, we'll highly recommend a series of tips booklets to demonstrate your expertise on a related topic without having to write and publish an entire book.

For example, Steve Kaye (http://www.SteveKaye.com) wrote a book on meetings called *Meetings in an Hour or Less*. He has created credibility on the topic and although the book is superb and gets rave reviews, not everybody feels they have time to read an entire book about conducting effective meetings.

Steve enhanced the book by doing a tips booklet called *117 Tips for Effective Meetings*. He's established himself as an expert in conducting quick and efficient meetings plus he has a *take away* product that sell for $5 that most people will purchase if they don't buy the book.

He inexpensively creates these 16-page booklets (55¢ each) that contain the tips as well as promotional material for his books, seminars, and the offer to have the books custom printed for a fee.

Each booklet is 4¼"x8½" and contains 16 mini pages and a coated stock cover with a contrasting color of ink for the titling (for example red ink and white cover stock). You can create booklets in a word processor or any other publishing program that lets you work within the physical guidelines and send the camera-ready copy to the printer.

The guru of tips booklets is Paulette Ensign and her web site is http://www.tipsbooklets.com. Everything you need to know about writing your own booklets is available from this site.

The printer who specializes in printing these mini-gems is Kirkland printing. Contact them at 619-583-3676 to get a quote, samples, and delivery information.

If you want a template that you can use as a *cut and paste* model (including the cover), send an e-mail to Mike Rounds (Mike@RoundsMiller.com) and ask for the free tips booklet template. He'll e-mail you the template and instructions in Word. Once you have the template, remove the existing text and add your own. Then, it's off to the printers.

E-BOOKS

The latest delivery vehicle is to use the internet (or CD-ROM) to offer the reader a lot of information in a very efficient manner.

There are several schools of thought about the delivery of e-books that are determined by how much time you personally want to spend fulfilling the orders.

1. On one end of the spectrum, there are fully automated shopping cart delivery systems that allow the customer to order the book, pay for it with a credit card, download and read and/or print it out. The systems verifies the customer's credit card, deposits the money in your bank account, and delivers the material without you having to do anything other than spend the money and pay your taxes.

   The more exotic systems allow you to decide how many copies of the e-book the customer can download, whether it can be printed out, simply read on the screen, or whether the entire file can be downloaded and shared with others. You can get the information and software systems to automate the process from Rosetta (http://RosettaMachine.com) or Lightning Source, which also supplies print on demand (http://www.LightningSource.com).

2. On the other end of the scale, you can use your e-mail and create a totally manual system where the customer sends an e-mail request (along with a credit card number) and you send back the e-book as an e-mail attachment.

If you'd like to see how the latter works for FREE, go to http://www.MikeRounds.com and request a free mini e-book on tips for searching the internet. He'll send you the mini book in PDF format and you can print it out and use it to become the first kid on your block who can actually find something on the internet that they really want.

Whatever delivery vehicle you decide to use for your e-book, you must convert your material to the PDF format using Adobe Acrobat (http://www.adobe.com) before you send it if you want the system to be as trouble free as possible. Acrobat has pretty much become the de facto standard for sending documentation to anybody, anywhere, in an uncorrupted format.

The best description of Acrobat is a universal snapshot system that's extremely simple to use. After you have created the content for your e-book (text, graphics, and hyperlinks) using a program like Word, you press a button that commands Adobe Acrobat to take a snapshot of the entire file.

To convert your material you must first buy a copy of Acrobat writer. It's available for both Macintosh and Windows and costs about $250, and you can get it from http://www.Adobe.com

The software to read the files is free and now comes prepackaged with many major software programs. A standard practice is to post a notice with whatever you use and tell people that they can download the reader for FREE at http://www.Adobe.com.

Several firms have started offering free software to create PDF files. You can get their free downloads at http://www.daneprairie.com or http://www.pdf995.com.

That's all there is to it. The software converts the material to PDF (Portable Document Format), compresses it, adds the hyperlinks, and stores it. Once the file is stored as a PDF, it can be sent as an e-mail attachment, put on a floppy disk or CD-ROM, or stored on a web site for automatic download.

Once the customer receives it, the PDF file can be read, printed, stored, or copied by either a Macintosh or Windows computer that has the FREE reader software installed. Because the Acrobat program takes a virtual snapshot of the material in the file, the process doesn't care whether it's looking at high-resolution graphics or plain courier 10 texts.

PUBLIC DOMAIN MATERIAL

There's a whole world of material that's FREE to use that you can charge for by compiling it and using it as support material for your programs. All material generated by the government whether federal, state, or municipal is public domain. Simply stated, you can reproduce and distribute it without any restrictions whatsoever.

The fee for this material is for your efforts to research, compile, reproduce, and make it available, and not for the original creation or authorship of the work.

For example, Mike offers a course on obtaining U.S. Government Small Business Innovative Research (SBIR) grants. The course material fee is $30 and includes 30 pages of class notes plus a CD-ROM that contains PDF files with over 300 pages of material plus links and references to an additional 8,000 pages of reference, financial, and support material. He spent weeks researching the material and compiling it into a simple, easy-to-use CD-ROM.

The material is well worth the $30 price because the attendees would have to invest weeks of their own time in locating the materials. His charge for the public domain material covers his efforts in researching it plus the reproduction costs.

Matthew Lesco (http://www.governmentgrant.com) has been making a fortune for many years with his books on government giveaways. His technique is to write an outline of what the government has to offer in the way of grants and other government sponsored programs. He then researches what's currently available, where to find them, and the basics of how to apply for them, and includes material that the government has generated in his manual. Matthew actually writes very little of the material other than the outline, recommendations and conclusions, but he's allowed to reproduce and distribute the government's material in his book for free because it's public domain.

NOTES AND WORKSHEETS

Most consulting assignments and especially those speaking engagements that are training sessions will require some form of notes, handouts, or worksheets.

Here's where you can get clever and make money with your handouts by using them as the foundation for your workbooks. Simply expand the notes, outlines, and guidelines to create your workbooks. You've got the outline complete and all you have to do is fill-in the specifics. If you really want an easy way to do it, tape record your presentation and have it transcribed.

You can create a cover and have them spiral bound for couple of bucks at Office Depot (http://www.OfficeDepot.com) or other similar locations. Once they are bound, they can be sold for $20-$100 depending on the content and perceived value.

REPORTS AND REFERENCE MATERIAL

If your business career has been anything like Mike's, you've probably generated more reports than you care to remember. The reason you generated them was because the job required it and money, though highly overrated, was a driving factor in keeping your job so you decided to capitulate and do what the boss dictated.

And, just like Mike's reports, yours were probably greeted with a "thanks, what took you so long?" and thrown onto a pile with other material that never actually got read, utilized, or implemented.

But now, you can actually charge your clients for the hard work and diligence you put into those lengthy volumes of creative material. Dr. Pete Johnson, (http://www.strategicplanning.com) charges his clients for a combination of research, training sessions, and the reports he creates as a part of the program. Pete is one of the most successful consultant speakers we've ever met. His reports and their implementation will make the difference between the success and failure of his clients.

Here are some ground rules for successfully creating reports that you can sell to your clients:

- They must be 100 percent accurate—your clients are not only paying for the accuracy, they're going to use the material in the report to adjust their actions so it must be accurate.

- They can be lengthy—this is probably the one place in your career where you cannot write too much. Reports, by their very nature, are supposed to go into as much detail and minutiae as needed to get the points across and to explain everything that needs to be done to achieve success.

- They can be self-generated or a compilation of others material as long as you have permission or they are public domain.

- They can contain or include interviews of experts in the field.

- They can also contain: statistical reviews, databases, mailing lists and other resources.

- They can be sets of useful materials for example sample sales letters or sample contracts. Steve Stewart (http://www.steve-stewart.com) is the best real estate speaker we've ever known. Steve discovered that there are a ton of sales letters, forms, agreements, and other materials that real estate professionals need to support their sales efforts. Steve bundled up everything into several packages that have audiotape instructions and all the materials in both Windows and Macintosh format.

NEWSLETTERS

This is one of those areas where two people will give you four opinions as to whether or not it's **profitable** to write newsletters. Projects like newsletters take time and as a service provider, that's what you're selling. Make sure that there's a positive return on investment before you embark on one of these ventures.

Here's our opinion about newsletters based on observations and cash flow.

1. Newsletters are a good idea if:

   - You can get people to pay for a newsletter.

   - You're writing and distributing newsletters to keep your name and services in front of clients and/or prospects who can actually hire you.

   - You're using your newsletter as a forced method of compiling information that you plan to publish in the near future.

   - You can get sponsors to pay you (either cash or trade) to write and distribute your newsletter.

   - Your newsletter is getting you orders for your products or services.

2. Newsletters are not a good idea if:

   - You're writing them because your ego says you should.

   - You're not getting any business or referrals from them.

   - You're not making enough money to pay for the newsletter's hard costs plus your time.

- Somebody else who doesn't have to do the work said you should do it.

Notice that we did NOT discriminate or differentiate between paper or electronic newsletters. The uninformed will tell you that an e-newsletter is OK because it's virtually free to distribute compared to the printing, handling, and postage costs of a paper version.

The reality is that the publication has to show a profit for you or it's not worth writing and distributing it, regardless of the delivery method. Even if you break even on the hard costs, you're still throwing away your time and as we've already noted, it's the most valuable commodity you've got.

Tom Antion's e-mail newsletter (http://www.antion.com) is a great example of the right way to do it. He uses it to sell lots of products, advertise his world famous Butt Camp, and get loads of people to sign up for his tele-seminars. His return on investment is outstanding and his reputation as an expert in this field is growing with each issue.

Here's a special noteworthy consideration: if your industry is overcrowded with printed newsletters, consider producing an audio newsletter. Current costs are less than $1 per tape or CD, recorded, reproduced, and mailed, and these will surely get listened to, passed on, and remembered.

The formats can vary from articles read into the tape to a one-on-one interview with current industry leaders. If you're uncomfortable with this concept, professional tape duplicating businesses have lists of narrators who will record the materials for you.

ARTICLES

Here's another area of questionable return unless it's done properly. Writing articles is time consuming and seeing your name in print is a poor return on investment unless you're getting cash business in return.

We've written monthly columns for fee and free, and both have had mixed results. Editors, especially trade journal editors and those who publish industry specific newsletters, are in need of experts to write good, meaty articles that will enhance the credibility of their publication.

As a general rule, they really don't care about your investment of time and will appeal to your ego saying that "your efforts will enhance your credibility" because you're now published.

Re-read the pros and cons of newsletters on the previous page as they are equally appropriate here when writing articles.

Ed Rigsbee (http://www.rigsbee.com) taught us how to make writing articles pay off. He's made his fame and fortune with his partnering techniques and freely shares the techniques with others. Here's his secret to success with articles:

- Write articles for trade journals that represent the industry or discipline where you are likely to get hired.

- After you've written articles for a specific target industry, try to generalize the article and put them on your web site with permission to reprint them as long as you get the credit.

> Permission to reprint articles by _____ at no charge is granted with the agreement that the article bio be included following each article used and one copy of the publication in which the article is published be provided to _____. A fee of $300 per article will be expected for articles published without the closing bio and contact information.

- Notify anybody you think will be a good source of notoriety that the articles are available for reprint for FREE.

- Don't jump at the chance to write articles for somebody unless you can justify the investment in time.

The more exposure you gain through an organization's printed material, the more familiar you become. When it's time to hire a consultant, your name, your expertise, and perhaps your face will be a common element in their business experience.

ORGANIZATIONAL INVOLVEMENT

Of all the methods there are for promoting consulting services, nothing has ever proved to be more advantageous than joining an organization and getting involved.

Because consultants are hired for performance as opposed to presence, people with the power and authority to hire us need to be made aware of our skills, expertise, knowledge, and level of commitment to projects under our control.

Virtually all industries have numerous organizations (or associations) that can be advantageous to join. The key to success in this arena, however, is to not only join but to get involved with the organization.

People are curious about how others make their living, and no doubt you will have the opportunity to discuss your business and gain referrals. As society becomes more complex, membership in organizations becomes a way of meeting people with similar values and interests. The assumption is that prospects like to do business with people they know and trust.

The National Trade and Professional Associations Directory from Columbia Books (http://www.columbiabooks.com) list 7,500 national trade associations, professional societies and labor unions. Five convenient indices enable you to look up associations by subject, budget, geographic area, acronym and executive director. Other features include: contact information, serial publications, upcoming convention schedule, membership and staff size, budget figures, and background information.

Historically, there's no better way to get business than by networking with people and organizations that are in either a position to hire you or to refer you simply because they know you and have first-hand experience of your capabilities. The halls of business success are lined with stories about how networking, contacts, and connections have played a significant role in the success of business people everywhere. Here's Mike's story.

"I can attest to this success even though I was reluctant to get involved in the process. Anyhow, here's the story. In 1992 I ran into a speaking acquaintance who said that even though I was getting pretty good, I needed to get involved with the National Speakers Association (NSA)

I had two reasons why I didn't want to be come involved with a formal organization: I didn't like giving my time away and I didn't like the politics of organizations which is why I was working for myself.

Nevertheless he convinced me to join. Because of my level of expertise and success with speaking I had assumed that I was going to become the guiding light for speakers everywhere. Surprisingly, I didn't become the instant speaking guru I had envisioned. My first experience with the organization was so overwhelming that I considered changing my profession to a career in worm farming.

I went to Orlando, Florida to attend the NSA's convention. The opening keynote speaker was Og Mandino and the keynote lineup included Anthony Robbins, Zig Ziglar, and several other speakers who are household names. Couple that with dozens of breakout and seminar speakers who kept huge audiences enthusiastic about every business topic imaginable and I figured I'd gotten into a business where I was actually not very skilled.

After returning home, I theorized that since there were local chapters of the NSA, that if I couldn't be a big fish in a big puddle, I could be big fish at the local level so off I went to a symposium in Palm Springs, California. Guess what I'd forgotten? The speakers who appeared at the Convention belonged to local chapters. Fortunately two significant things occurred that saved my career:

- A couple of the speakers at the symposium weren't as good as I was so I figured that there might be a chance for me and,

- The chapter needed volunteers to help in areas where I had a lot of experience and background so I decided to get involved.

Voila! By volunteering I gave myself exposure to speakers and people in the industry who were already successful and over the next few months they began to know me, my name, what I did, and how good I was at doing it. Over time I became chapter president and was asked to present a breakout session for the NSA's Winter Workshop and then at the national convention.

While I was on the platform the recruiter for CareerTrack heard me speak and hired me right off the platform. I spent four years with CareerTrack as a lead trainer and was the very last program presenter in their lineup when the company was sold and dissolved in 2000.

The contacts, connections, friends, business acquaintances, and the business I have attained from my involvement in the NSA is virtually incalculable. In fact, over 50 percent of my revenues can probably be tracked to my joining and participating in one single organization, the NSA.

The chances are pretty good that you'll find one or more organizations that are prime candidates for the kinds of services you're currently offering. By getting involved with them, you'll be putting yourself and the services you offer in front of a viable audience to sample and purchase."

Chapter 6 Speaking

Speaking presents you with a unique opportunity to educate the public about your services while packaging the advertising program in either an entertaining or informational manner.

The National Speakers Association says that a professional speaker is an expert who speaks. That pretty much defines a consultant too but, based on results; a professional speaker is a person who makes a living through speaking. This means that if you speak to advertise and promote your services and get clients, you're a professional speaker because you profit (albeit indirectly) from your speaking efforts.

Speaking before a group of people can be rewarding, necessary and fun. Why you speak before a group of people is directly relevant to how you position yourself with your marketing materials.

There are three reasons to speak before an audience:

1.   To fill an immediate need (e.g. press conference about an oil spill).

2.   For fun or enjoyment (e.g. telling people about your hobby or passion).

3.   For profit (e.g. making more money than spending).

Realistically, most of your time is spent doing things other than speaking—traveling, writing, research, and more importantly, and marketing. By the time you're on the platform to finally speak, it's like a reward for all the preparation you've done up to that point.

WHERE'S THE MONEY?

There are three ways to make money from speaking. They are:

1. Fees. This is also known as the front side. This is the money the presenter receives for that speaking engagement. Speaking fees of $100 to $10,000 per day are commonplace for acknowledged industry experts. See page 31 for setting your fees. It has been reported that Les Brown former talk-show host makes $20,000 per speaking engagement; Stephen R. Covey

author of *Seven Habits of Highly Effective People* $75,000 per day; Dr. Phil the tough-loving doctor cashes in on the lecture circuit at more than $100,000 per speech, Tony Robbins infomercial star $125,000 per day; Bill Cosby stand-up comic and one of America's most beloved television stars makes $350,000 plus a private jet, and Jerry Seinfeld stand-up comedian and co-created of the hit TV sitcom Seinfeld in 1990 makes $600,000 for a speaking engagement.

2. Product. This is also known as BORS (back of room sales). Product sales are limited only to your imagination and include books, audio products, video products, t-shirts, mugs, postcards, posters, candy, bookmarkers, pen, pencils, forms, and jewelry. Some consultants, like real estate consultants, have been known to sell over $200,000 worth of BORS at a single seminar.

3. Backside. Anything that you are offering after the speech or seminar. The most common are consulting services but almost anything can be offered. We have an associate who conducts seminars on valuing a business for sale, loans, or public offering. He makes virtually nothing from the seminar itself due to the advertising costs and he has no support material (product). However, he averages about $500,000 per year in consulting services as a result of his speaking efforts. He uses the time to *information overload* the audience and then reminds them that *he's the pro* and it would probably be far more expeditious to hire him than to try and do it themselves.

TYPE OF PRESENTATIONS

There are several types of presentations and one is not better than another. However, it is important to know the difference because your marketing materials will be different for each.

A keynoter is a speaker that inspires, informs, motivates, entertains and/or educates. Usually, keynote presentations are 1-2 hours in length. Typically, the speaking slots are opening general sessions or closing general sessions at conventions, organizational rallies, or retreats. General sessions are for all the attendees.

Trainers share a specific, targeted message that is designed to impart to the participants knowledge that is of immediate or long-term value. Typically, the speaking slots are seminars, workshops, trainings, or breakouts.

If you're considering professional speaking as a career, remember the following:

1. Keynote speakers are known for who they are and to be a successful keynoter, you must create a recognizable reputation and personality that people are interested in and are willing to pay for.

2. Trainers are known first, and foremost, for the topics they speak about or the subjects that they address. Most successful speakers, whether they end up as keynoters or trainers, start out as trainers because until your name and reputation are widely known, it is what you speak about that will be of the most interest to clients rather than who you are.

PRIVATE SEMINAR AND WORKSHOP COMPANIES

Our first commentary about this venue is a wonderful quote from fellow speaker Steve Kaye, PhD (http://www.stevekaye.com): "Public seminar companies are NOT havens for the unemployable."

We've heard speakers make the comment that "business is slow so they'd be willing to give the seminar companies a few days of their time to fill the gaps." Let's get real—the seminar companies are in business to make a profit and they are a real, full-time business—even if they aren't to you! This means that they, not you, will decide on who works for them and under what terms and conditions they will use your speaking services—if at all!

Mike spent four years as a lead trainer for CareerTrack, which means he created training programs as well as delivered them. The time he spent with them was a precious experience because it allowed him the opportunity to experience, first hand, what a Road Warrior goes through to deliver high content programs to the public.

Qualities seminar companies look for in trainers:

1. Lively, compelling training style speakers with excellent platform skills.

2. High content information to provide audiences with skills and insights, and the motivation to apply them. Seminar attendees want lots of how-to's as well as entertainment and motivation.

3. Individuals that can provide their real-life stories to fill in the material from the seminar company's manual.

4. Love of the show. You must LOVE to get up in front of an audience, and BE THE SHOW, day after day, four or five times a week, delivering the same program. You must have the ability to make the program sound fresh and new each time you present it.

5. Ability to sell. Most of the seminar companies sell back of room products (audio/videotapes and books) and/or in-house programs generated by the

interest in the seminar. These avenues of sales are highly profitable, and the ability to consistently sell these products is so important that if your sales revenues drop, your chances of the seminar company rebooking you decreases rapidly.

FEES

Honorarium: $250 to $1,000 per day. Most companies pay for your airline ticket, hotel, and car rental.

Per Diem: $40 to $100 per day for meals, tips, and any other incidentals.

On-site Programs: The same honorarium as a seminar—some seminar companies pay $200 to $500 more.

Product Sales: Between 5 to 20 percent commissions on sales of back of room product.

Programs per Month: You will be required to deliver 8 to 15 seminars a month, and 2 and 5 on-sites each month.

PROCEDURE FOR HIRING TRAINERS

Hiring procedures differ from company to company. However, almost all seminar companies request the following in order to consider you for a position as a trainer.

- A one-page letter stating the topics you present, your training experience, and the reasons you wish to train for that company.

- A standard resume listing your educational backgrounds, professional credentials, and work-related experience. Some seminar companies ask you to submit a color photo.

- A 90-minute (up to a 6-hour) videotape (seminar companies differ in actual length of time they want) showing you in action.

If the company is interested after reviewing all you have sent them, they will call you for a phone interview. After the phone interview, you may be invited to company headquarters to audition, or you may be asked to prepare another videotape using one of their workbooks.

If your audition goes well, or your second videotape is reviewed favorably, you will be offered a contract. Go over the contract carefully, point by point, to make sure you understand and agree to everything in the contract. It is written for the protection of both you and the company.

THE PITFALLS

All leads that you get from seminars while delivering one of their seminars must go back to the seminar company. You cannot use these leads. However, you can list the in-house companies that you worked for in your promotional materials.

Constant travel can be very fatiguing, leaving you no time or energy to market yourself. This leads to the situation of lagging behind on the marketing necessary to promote yourself when you do venture out on your own.

You represent the company—it is neither about you or your company.

The venue for the seminar companies are straight forward, but it's not something that most speakers want to attempt. You'll find a partial list of the seminar companies. The ones listed are currently active and might be looking for trainers in your area of expertise.

SEMINAR COMPANY ADDRESSES

AHRD Association, Inc
Project Mgmt Mentor Div
2082 Union St
San Francisco CA 94123-4103

American Biographical Inst Inc
5126 Bur Oak Cir
PO Box 31226
Raleigh NC 27622
919-781-8710

American Mgmt Assn
1601 Broadway
New York NY 10019
212-586-8100

American Productivity and
Quality Ctr
123 N Post Oak Ln
Houston TX 77024
713-681-4020

Assn of Natl Advertisers Inc
155 E 44th St
New York NY 10017
212-697-5950

Boston Center of Adult Ed
5 Commonwealth
Boston MA 02116
617-267-4430 x 715

Brookings Institute
Ctr for Public Policy Education
1775 Massachusetts Ave NW
Washington DC 20036
202-797-6000

Bryant College
The Ctr for Mgmt Development
450 Douglas Pike
Smithfield RI 02917-1283
401-232-6200

Burke Institute; The
805 Central Avenue
Cincinnati OH 45202
800-543-8635
513-684-4999
513-684-7733 fax
http://www.burkeinstitute.com
BurkeInstitute@BurkeInstitute.com

CA Institute of Technology
Industrial Relations Ctr
I-90
Pasadena CA 91125
626-395-6592

Center for Business
Development
2409 Villa Ln
McHenry IL 60050-2969
815-344-2500

Center for Creative Leadership
5000 Laurinda Dr
Greensboro NC 27410
336-288-7210

Center for Creative Learning
2437 N Booth St
Milwaukee WI 53212-2930
414-873-6040

Clemson University College of
Commerce & Industry
PO Drawer 912
Clemson SC 29633
864-646-2130

College of St Thomas
The Mgmt Ctr
Mail Station 5058
Saint Paul MN 55105
651-962-5860

Columbia Executive Programs
Columbia University
324 Uris Hall
New York NY 10027
212-854-3395

Computer Security Institute
600 Harrison St
San Francisco CA 94107
866-271-8529

Conference Board
845 3rd Ave
New York NY 10022
212-759-0900

Cornell University
NY State School of Industrial &
Labor Relations
16 E 34th St 4th Flr
New York NY 10016
212-340-2800

Ctr for Accelerated Learning
1103 Wisconsin St
Lake Geneva WI 53147
Dimensional Reading Inc
98 Main St Ste 539
Tiburon CA 94920
415-435-3875

Disney World Seminar
Productions
PO Box 10000
Lake Buena Vista FL
32830-1000
407-824-7997

Evolving Technology Institute
PO Box 60010
San Diego CA 92106-2095
800-325-1289

Federal Publications Inc
901 15th St NW Ste 1010
Washington DC 20005-2351

Foundation for Credit Education
RD 1
692 Brandywine Rd
Nazareth PA 18064

Fred Pryor Seminars &
CareerTrack
9757 Metcalf Ave
Overland Park KS 66212-2219
800-780-8476
trainerinfo@pryor.com

Human Dynamics
PO Box 7241
Greensboro NC 27417
336-854-0120

Institute for Professional
Education
PO Box 756
Arlington VA 22216
703-527-8700

Institute of Mgmt Consultants
2025 M St NW Ste 800
Washington DC 20036-3309
202-367-1134 800-221-2557
202-367-2134
http://www.imcusa.org

Interface Group Inc; The
300 1st Ave
Needham MA 02194
508-746-2907

Intl Business and Mgmt Inst
PO Box 3172
Tustin CA 92681-3271

Intl Business Information
Services
Drawer 4082
Irvine CA 92716-4082

Intl Registry of Org Development
Profess
11234 Walnut Ridge Rd
Chesterland OH 44026

J L Kellogg Graduate School of
Mgmt
Northwestern University
2169 Sheraton Rd
Evanston IL 60208-2800

Karrass Negotiating, Mgmt and
Sales Seminars
8370 Wilshire Blvd Ste 300
Beverly Hills CA 90211-2333
323-951-7500

Kepner-Tregoe Inc
Research Rd
PO Box 704
Princeton NJ 08542
609-921-2806

Kroeger Associates
3605-C Chain Bridge Rd
Fairfax VA 22030
703-591-6284

Lakewood Conferences
50 S 9th St
Minneapolis MN 55402
612-333-0471

Leadership Development
Associates
2255 Fields McGrage Dr
Canton GA 30114

Learning Annex
16 E 53 St 4th Flr
New York NY 10022
212-371-0280
212-319-1623 fax

Learning Connection
201 Wayland Ave
Providence RI 02906
401-274-9330

Market Data Retrieval
1 Forest Pkwy
Shelton CT 06484-0947
800-243-5538

Mgmt Directions
1250 Old Henderson Rd
Columbus OH 43220

MTS Systems Corp
1400 Technology Dr
Eden Prairie MN 55344
952-937-4000

National Businesswomen's
Leadership Association
6901 W 63rd St
Shawnee Mission KS 66201-1349
913-432-7755

National Seminar Group
Rockhurst University
Continuing Education Ctr Inc
PO Box 419107
Kansas City MO 64141-6107
913-432-7755 800-258-7246
913-432-0824
http://www.natsem.com

Natl Assn of Credit Mgmt
(NACM)
8840 Columbia 100 Pkwy Ste
100
Columbia MD 21045-2158
410-740-8311

Natl Crisis Prevention Inst
3315-K N 124h St
Brookfield WI 53005-9932
262-783-5787

Natl Seminars Group
6901 W 63rd St 3rd Flr
Overland Park KS 66202
800-258-7246

Ned Hermann Group; The
2075 Buffalo Creek Rd
Lake Lure NC 28746

Northwestern University
1936 Sheridan Rd
Evanston IL 60208-4040
847-491-5665

Novations Consulting Group
5314 N 250 W Ste 320
Provo UT 84601
801-375-7525

NTL Institute
300 N Lee St
Alexandria VA 22314
703-548-1500

NY University School of
Continuing Education
Ctr for Direct Marketing
48 Cooper Sq
New York NY 10003
800-346-3698

Organizational Consultants Inc
55 Child St Ste 301
San Francisco CA 94133

Padgett Thompson (AMA)
800-255-4141

Penn State Executive Programs
310 Business Administration
Bldg
University Park PA 16801-9975
814-865-3435

Personnel Decisions Inc
2000 Plaza VII Tower
45 S 7th St
Minneapolis MN 55402-1608
612-339-0927

Pope and Associates Inc
1313 E Kemper Rd Ste 350
Cincinnati OH 45246
513-671-1277

Power and Systems
PO Box 388
Prudential Station
Boston MA 02199
617-437-1640

Princeton Research Institute
PO Box 2702
Scottsdale AZ 85252

Psychological Associates Inc
8201 Maryland Ave
Saint Louis MO 63105
314-862-9300

Rice University
Office of Executive Development
Jesse H Jones Graduate School
of Administration MS 531
6100 Main St
Houston TX 77005
713-348-4838

Robert Yourzak and Associates
7320 Gallagher Dr Ste 325
Minneapolis MN 55435
952-831-2235

SkillPath Seminars
Faculty Trainer
6900 Squibb Rd Ste 300
Mission KS 66202
660-646-9933
mailto:recruit@skillpath.net
http://www.skillpath.com

Southern Illinois University
Ctr for Mgmt Studies
Edwardsville IL 62026-1251
618-650-2166

Swan Consultants Inc
420 Lexington Ave
New York NY 10170
212-517-9818

Sys-tem-a-tion
2095 S Pontiac Way
Denver CO 80224
800-747-9783

Teleometrics Intl
4567 Lake Shore Dr
Waco TX 76710-1814

Tennant
PO Box 1452 MS 200
Minneapolis MN 55440
763-540-1200

Thomas Wilds Associates Inc
PO Box 11120
Greenwich CT 06830

Trancorp
20200 Governors Dr
Olympia Fields IL 60461
708-481-2900

TREC Software Enterprises Corp
31220 La Baya Dr Ste 110
Westlake Village CA 91362

Tri-Unity Wellness Ctr
629 Spruce St
Madison WI 53715

Tustin Technical Institute Inc
3887 State St Ste 210
Santa Barbara CA 93105
805-682-7171

UCLA Extension
10995 Le Conte Ave
Los Angeles CA 90024

United Communications Group
CCMI
1300 Rockville Pike
Rockville MD 20852-3030
800-487-4824

Univ of AZ
Engineering Professional
Development
PO Box 9
Harvill Bldg
Tucson AZ 85721

Univ of MI; The
MI Business School
Executive Education Ctr
Ann Arbor MI 48019-1234

Univ of Pittsburgh
Joseph M Katz Graduate School
of Business
Ctr for Executive Education
253 Cathedral of Learning
Pittsburgh PA 15260

Univ of Richmond
Mgmt Institute
E Claiborne Robins School of
Business
Richmond VA 23173
804-289-8019

Univ of WI
Mgmt Institute
The School of Business
432 N Lake St
Madison WI 53706-1498
608-262-3089

Univ of WI—Milwaukee
University Outreach
161 W Wisconsin Ste 600
Milwaukee WI 53203
414-227-3320

University Continuing Education
Association
1 Dupont Cir Ste 615
Washington DC 22036
202-659-3130

World Trade Institute
1 World Trade Ctr 55th Flr
New York NY 10048

Wright State University
College of Continuing and
Communications Education
140 E Monument Ave
Dayton OH 45402

Chapter 7 Rubber Chicken Circuit

The Rubber Chicken Circuit is a traditional venue for putting your services in front of a live audience and includes such organizations as Rotary Clubs (http://www.rotary.org/services/clubs/index.html) Lions Clubs, Kiwanis Clubs (http://www.Kiwanis.org), Chambers of Commerce (http://www.USChamber.com), churches, senior retirement communities, civic events or any organization that meets on a regular basis (weekly, monthly, every other month or quarterly) which typically does not have a budget to pay speakers and is willing to provide a meal for you when you speak. Once you become a regular on this circuit, you will soon understand why it is called rubber chicken.

Traditionally, other than the free meal (yecch!) they do NOT pay anything, may NOT allow you to sell your materials, and usually object to you asking for their mailing list. However, ask if there is a budget for speaking. There might be a small amount available.

Why then, you ask, would you ever want to speak before a group like this? The answer is lots of reasons including:

1. A live audience to practice your new material.

2. A place to demonstrate your material for a meeting planner in the area in front of a live audience.

3. A place to get audio and video recordings with a live audience.

4. A place to make your services known, either directly to the attendees or through referrals.

5. Sometimes, you can offer products for sale.

6. And sometimes, you can get the organization's roster and mail your materials to them.

Most speakers go back to the Rubber Chicken Circuit at different times in their career. Can you imagine if Tom Peters or Les Brown were to offer a free program, whether it was untried material or not, what kind of attendance the organization would get? It's a win-win situation for everyone.

GETTING EXPERIENCE

If you are a beginner in front of a group, or if you have only given presentations to the Toastmasters Club or within your organization, by using the Rubber Chicken Circuit, you can get experience speaking before a live audience of people who don't already know you.

The booking process is simple but not easy because you have to play by their rules. You can get our videotape, *Talk, Talk, Talk* that explains the process and all of the benefits in detail at http://www.RoundsMiller.com but in the meantime, here's the short course on getting booked:

First and foremost remember their rules:

1. Follow their rules, regulations and guidelines regarding promoting products and services. This is NOT an infomercial. You are their entertainment for the meeting.

2. Arrive early, get set up, schmooze with the people who attend, and plan to stay for 10-15 minutes after the program to schmooze some more.

3. You will be given approximately 20-25 minutes to speak, answer questions, and finish up. After that, you'll start to see the members walking out on you because you're encroaching on their time. If there are numerous announcements that day, your time might be reduced. One time, Nancy was speaking at a service club and there were no announcements so she had almost 45 minutes. Be flexible!

4. If possible, collect business cards, survey cards with contact information, or anything else that will allow you to get in touch with the attendees.

When Mike was program chair for his Rotary club, he had some great speakers from the National Speakers Association who came and spoke for free as a favor. Some of the most entertaining and enlightening speakers as well as the best-received speakers didn't get any interest or leads at all.

Some speakers got a couple, and some speakers were swamped with requests for additional information about their availability, fees, and additional programs or consulting services. This is no different than any other advertising or promotion venue—it's a numbers game and sometimes the numbers are higher than others. In other words, don't expect miracles!

Look in the local phone directories for the clubs that you want to address. If you prefer to not use the paper version, go to http://www.bigbook.com or http://www.switchboard.com and type in Rotary Clubs, Lions Clubs, or whatever organization you're looking to book.

One of the great things about these organizations is that most of them use post office boxes because the officers and directors change each year. This means that your mailing list will be accurate and you won't get a lot of returned material.

Make a mailing to the clubs and organizations announcing your availability and topic. One option for mailing is to prepare a one-sheet description on your talk that's specifically designed for a 20-minute talk. Make sure that you include all of your contact information so they can get a hold of you day or night. You may want to mention that you are available for *last minute* cancellations in case the scheduled speaker becomes sick or is out of town.

We've found that four-color postcards work about as well as the full one-sheet and they're inexpensive (500 four-color cards for $125). Contact Nancy Miller at 310-544-9502 (http://www.roundsmiller.com) and order a copy of *Marketing with Postcards*. It's $39.95 and will give you a ton of information about design, content, and all the resources for graphics and printing you'll ever need.

The best time to make a mailing is in June because most of the organizations change leadership July 1. The new program chair is trying to line up their year and is full of energy. The second best time to make a mailing is in December/January. The other half of the organizations change leadership January 1 or the program chair only had enough energy to schedule half the year and about December/January they are looking for speakers again.

SHOWCASE

If you have potential clients in the audience, the program is known as a showcase and its primary purpose, other than to dazzle the audience with your skills and knowledge, is to demonstrate or sample your skills to the potential client so they can be impressed and hire you for scads of money.

There are a lot of full fee speaking engagements that result from the exposure that people have gained on the Rubber Chicken Circuit. Sampling your skills is the most valuable tool in your arsenal and this is definitely a way to let people get a free sample.

Some examples of showcases are sponsored by a bureau before their clients or speaking at an association meeting of meeting planners. A showcase is any group of people that could individually hire you such as YPO (the Young Presidents' Organization http://www.YPO.org) or the Million Dollar Roundtable in real estate.

BACK OF ROOM SALES (BORS)

Because the Rubber Chicken Circuit hears a lot of speakers (weekly in some instances), they tend to grow thick skin and don't like to be hustled. If you have a product or service to sell, ask the program chair if you can have it available that day or if you can pass out a flyer. Let the chair know that your talk will not be a 20-30 minute commercial about how great you are.

Another way of encouraging the program chair to say yes to your selling product at the meeting is to offer (and let the group know) that 10-20 percent of the proceeds will be donated to the club's favorite charity.

If you have a product or service that you would like to offer to the organization, don't ask the program chair for the club's roster. Many are unwilling to give the roster out for purposes of junk mailing or telemarketing.

Stop by an office supply store and buy a brightly colored 9"x12" envelope. At the beginning of your presentation, let the group know that you are going to have a drawing for a book (or tape). Use your own product if you have one, or stop by a bookstore and purchase a book that is closely related to the topic that you are speaking on that day. Ask those that would like to participate in the drawing to simply drop a business card into the envelope.

About five minutes before you conclude, draw a winner. This is a wonderful technique for several reasons.

1. The person who won the book will open it up and start looking at it (during your presentation). When the winner gets back to the table, the people on both sides and around the table will strain to see what the book is about. You have created a feeding frenzy for book buying.

2. The remaining business cards are carefully put in a pocket and you will be following up either in writing, e-mail or calling. This is better than the members' roster because the people that attended the presentation now know you and hopefully they will love you.

To obtain some advance publicity and help bolster the attendance at your program (hopefully with possible clients) is to offer to write an article (or series of articles) for their newsletter before and/or after you speak. Newsletter editors are often overworked, underpaid and have little editorial support. By volunteering to write an article that helps them out, you'll get a lot of support and cooperation (not to mention exposure with the group).

To make it easy on yourself, you can re-purpose some of the articles that you have written before and applying the specific examples to the organization or you can use this opportunity to make yourself write articles. You're not writing *War and Peace*! Short articles (200-400 words), checklists, surveys and the like are very popular and easy to insert into any format.

CHURCHES

This venue is where you might not get paid and then again, you might. We have occasionally spoken for a church group but some speakers make this venue their primary market. Churches have groups of people who are interested in lots of things that speakers address. The key is to find the right topics and the right audiences. The venue isn't limited to the pulpit. There are Sunday School programs, fundraisers, retreats, conferences, Wednesday evening program, single programs, couple programs, parent programs, etc.

Like the rest of the Rubber Chicken Circuit, churches offer the potential of clients in the audience. They may or may not encourage you to offer your books and materials to their congregation and to stick around and schmooze with the attendees.

Churches often pay for training, but not as well as a Fortune 500 company does. Their budgets are smaller and sometimes, if you speak for the congregation, you'll receive what's known as a love offering. (They'll pass the plate and if the audience loves you, you'll get a few bucks!) You may receive the whole offering or split it with the church.

The process for booking them can be one of two ways:

1. Use the exact system described for booking the Rubber Chicken Circuit.

2. Use a modified version of the technique by locating the churches and calling to qualify them before you send out your materials.

Regardless of how you get booked, get a letter saying how good you were from the senior pastor and ask for referrals. Put this in your media kit. A referral from another pastor is very important in this venue.

LIBRARIES

Yes boys and girls, libraries are still with us even though the internet has threatened to dominate the world with its vast expanse of electronic publications. But libraries are a place to speak.

Contact the libraries and see if they will sponsor your program. Contact the media and see if they will tape the program for local PAT (Public Access Television or cable) airing, and make sure that you get a copy of the edited videotape from the program.

The Los Angeles Public Library audiotapes every program we do and gives us the master tape. We also sell our products in the library bookstore the day of the seminar. One time, they made arrangements with LA City View (cable) to tape one of Mike's programs. They made the library look like the Tonight Show with a five-camera shoot. We received a master tape and the rights to reproduce it as our own product and they got the rights to air it locally.

Nancy was paid to deliver her Clutterology program and encouraged to sell books and tapes at the library as a community event charging $5 per person. The library's meeting room could only hold 85 people and they had an overflow of 50 additional people. She ended up doing a second fee paid program, and once again sold books and tapes. The most exciting thing was that to advertise the program, the library had an ad on a bus bench!

Libraries have several different types of venues. There are staff sessions, public seminars, Friends of the Library sponsored seminar, book reading/signing seminar, children programs and fundraisers.

SENIOR CITIZENS COMMUNITIES

With the graying of the baby boomers, more speaking opportunities for retirement communities are becoming available. Contact the local senior citizens communities and see if they will sponsor your program. Contact the video club in the community and see if they will tape the program for local PAT (Public Access Television) airing. Make sure that you get a copy of the edited videotape from the program.

We have done programs for Leisure World, sold tapes and books, and got a fully edited video of the program. The senior citizens made sure the video got aired on local cable and we got the notoriety.

When you book any of these venues, contact the local newspapers, bureaus, meeting planners, or anyone you think might be a possible client and invite them to the program. You'll never know when one or more of these will open up the floodgates for a raft of speaking or training leads and the publicity is always good for your media kit.

Chapter 8 Rubber Band Circuit

For all practical purposes, these are adult schools, community colleges, state colleges, and universities where, if you have a winning class, will continue to book you until you feel you have been stretched to your limit, which is why it is called the Rubber Band Circuit.

Consultants can use the Rubber Band Circuit very effectively. If you're looking for individuals to hire you, but you don't have a large budget for advertising, this circuit provides the opportunity to get before people and still make some money for the effort.

However, the students are not your prisoners. The information in the seminar must be able to stand on its own. Don't lock the students in the classroom until they make an appointment with or hire you. Instead, show them how simple it is by how much knowledge, confidence, and experience you have, and how much easier it would be to hire you rather than do it themselves.

If you have a hot topic, it's easy to get booked here but be aware that schools have between a three to nine month window from the time you submit your class outline until the date you give the seminar.

FEES

Each school does things a little differently, but there are some basic similarities.

EMPLOYEE

The fees for hourly rate are $20-$50 per hour. Payment is usually received 30-90 days after the class. Typically, if you are being paid on an hourly basis, you are considered an employee and have a lot of paperwork to fill out.

You'll be required to complete a series of questionnaires complete with work history, educational background, and references and probably be required to sign an oath of allegiance to the United States. You'll also be requested to observe and report any apparent violations of child abuse. (Yes, we know your classes are only for adults!)

They may automatically enroll you in some sort of retirement plan like APPLE Plan (which is a Social Security alternative retirement program chosen for part-time, temporary and seasonal employees) or PARS (Public Agency Retirement System). As we have been teaching at 30 different schools within California, we have numerous APPLE Plans and PARS accounts. What's really sad is that one account has a total of $4.94 after five years of contributions. Don't plan to make any of their plans your retirement nest egg.

Be prepared to be fingerprinted for the school file. Sometimes, we can go to someone in our community for an inked fingerprinting and just send the card to the school. A new system is called a Live Scan. No more black inked fingers. The fingerprints are scanned using a computer system and then e-mailed to the Department of Justice. The results are sent to the school. Some schools have the equipment; some schools use their local police department.

Some schools will allow you to use a local police department for a Live Scan. The cost is between $32 to $40. Each school creates a file that belongs to them and therefore you need to be fingerprinted each and every time you add another school.

You will need a Tuberculosis test. A TB test can be good for several years. We learned the hard way and seemed to be getting a shot every other day. We now ask for a copy of the test and other districts honor the document.

You may also be required to show up for a personal interview. We swear that all they want to see is that you are alive and breathing. During the interview, typically they outline the structure of the school and describe their policies. As we are geographically undesirable (over 100 miles) in some instances, the school has compromised with a telephone interview. There have been some schools where they demanded that we show up for the interview before they would even begin talking to us.

Typical also is two forms of photo identification. We use our current driver's license and passport. Again, depending on the distance we are from the school, some of the schools have accepted a photocopy of these documents.

The school will want a copy of your resume or professional vita'. You don't need to make this heavy duty or a masterpiece, but the schools do like to have this document on file.

If these elements seem objectionable to you and fly in the face of your freedoms or logic, don't be upset because you have a choice—either capitulate with the rules or forget about working in the venue. Period!

INDEPENDENT CONTRACTOR

The other method of compensation is a split of the class fee. The school and the presenter split the income of the class. The range is from 35 percent to 60 percent. 40 percent to the instructor is common. Typically, if you are being paid a split, your status is as an independent contractor.

For example: if there were 20 students @ $40 per person, that's $800 in fees. The instructor gets 40 percent or $320.

Sometimes, the school will take out their expenses before the split. Ask the school what expenses are charged to the seminar. Many times they include insurance, room rental, catalog space, etc.

Some schools will pay for the total number of registered students. If a student doesn't show up, you will still be compensated. Other schools will only pay you for those that showed up in the classroom. Many schools have a no refund policy (especially three days prior to the event) and even if the student doesn't show up, the student still paid for the course.

MATERIAL FEE

Back of Room Sales (BORS) can make the classes worth the time. The books in our example are $20 each so that's an additional $400 in your bank account. BORS can be optional or mandatory.

Some of the schools require that they collect the materials fee and then we invoice them and the schools sends us a check. Some schools may require that you send them a sample of the materials so they have a copy on file.

> A $20 materials fee "Marketing the One-Person Business 2nd Edition, #1-891440-29-2" is payable at the door.

CLASS COST

Usually, the continuing education or community service department will ask what we think the cost of the class should be. We usually defer to the experience and knowledge of the school. Ask what is common for the school. The schools are in business in their local community and know what their attendees are likely to pay for a class.

For instance, we have had the same seminar at different locations and the seminar fee varies. At an adult school, the cost might be $29. At a community college, the cost might be $29-$79. At a state college, the cost might be between $79-$99, and at a university, the cost might be $129-$249.

SUBMISSIONS

Instructors are selected on the basis of their education, credentials and, more often, work-related experience. We have found the easiest way to contact the schools is to send a package of information in the mail and then follow up. The envelope includes a cover letter, a class description, a resume or author bio and a reply postcard.

COVER LETTER

In the cover letter you are submitting, include any information that is currently not on other paperwork. Have you given this seminar previously? If so, how many people attended? What fee per individual was charged? Are you willing to do additional advertising beyond the school's advertising? An e-mail announcement from your database? The bottom line—how is the school going to make money off of your seminar?

Is there something in the media that makes this topic **hot** now! If so, let the school know about it so both you and they can capitalize on it.

Title

A good title can mean the difference between a program that pulls and one that doesn't live up to its potential. The title is one of the most important components of your program description and is your first chance to catch the reader's interest.

Exciting titles draw more people to a session than a dull one so the best titles are short, action-oriented, and use concise and powerful words.

Try to make the title as short as possible. Avoid those colons, as in "A Westerfield Happening: The Life and Times of J. Arthur Westerfield, Jr." Pick the title on either side of the colon.

Make the title action-oriented. That is best achieved by including a verb or its equivalent in the title. For example, for a session on the founding fathers of the town, a Nebraska teacher called it "Who's buried on Boot Hill?"

Use simple words, and try substituting a powerful word for a more commonly used word. Power words are those that excite people, such as save, free and discover. Instead of interesting, try savvy. Instead of meaningful, try significant. To find thousands of simple and power-packed words, consult Roget's Thesaurus.

Make the course title interactive. For example, a course title such as "Dental Facts" effectively describes the course content. But the same course called "Everything You Always Wanted to Ask Your Dentist" immediately forces the reader to become involved with the course description.

Ask the reader a question. "What Do We Know About Cholesterol?" demands an answer and is an excellent way to get a mental response from your readers. Use this technique sparingly, or your readers will become befuddled by too many unanswered questions.

Make the course title personal. The easiest way to do this is to use the word **you** in the title. "It's Up to You to Lose Weight" is an effective description for a class on taking personal responsibility for weight management. "What to Say After You Clear Your Throat" is an innovative and personal title for a class on dating. Don't get too clever with the title or it may miss the point.

Use familiar phrases that have positive connotations. This is an effective technique because the reader immediately makes a positive association with the class based on recall of the phrase used in positive situations in the past. One good example is "Movers and Shakers," a title for a dance-exercise class.

Identify the target audience in the course title. "Coping With Change: The Sandwich Generation" focuses on life management skills. However, instead of marketing to all who experience change, the title identifies those who find themselves becoming the caretakers for both their children and their parents.

Create a sense of reader identification. By writing titles that recall universal experiences, the reader will feel a personal identification with the topic and is more likely to respond to the program. The "One Minute Manager" speaks to the universal experience of today's high-pressure, hectic society.

Use quantitative titles or state the specific outcomes of participation in the program. "Ten Ways to Turn Out Terrific Kids" and "Fruitful Friction" are some examples. Notice that a title implying or stating an outcome includes a verb.

Use humor. Making people laugh is a good way to get them involved and to create a positive feeling about a program.

Create a sense of curiosity and fun or a sense of discovery and unique experience. "Are There Skeletons in Your Closet?" is an interesting title for an anatomy refresher. "Don't Drink the Water" turns the reader's attention to water pollution issues.

Keep program titles simple, non-threatening, and positive. "Promoting Cardiopulmonary Resuscitation—Level B" can be potentially intimidating. Instead, "You Can Save a Life with CPR" avoids jargon and puts the course in everyday terms.

Description

By making the session description short, action and benefit-oriented, and geared toward your participants and their needs, you'll find more people attending your session, and you'll have a clearer idea of the session's objectives and end results.

There are usually two preferred styles of description that will be listed in the catalog. The first style is a maximum of 30 words. Edit your copy including your bio to 30 words.

The second style longer copy with the description a maximum of a half-page. Write in short sentences and bullet points. When you find yourself writing extended sentences, simply put in a period and turn your thought into two or three sentences. After writing three sentences, start a new paragraph.

If you have a series of ideas or points, count them. Then include the number in the description. For example, "Find out the five latest theories on the formation of the universe," or "Discover the advantages of the seven most-used managerial techniques of executives in the Fortune 500."

Edit and rewrite the description once or twice to polish it and fine-tune the wording. It is well worth the effort.

Avoid starting the description, "In this session" or "This session will." Try not to refer to the participants in the third person, such as "the participants will." Eliminate unnecessary or unconvincing information. For example, "Using the flip chart, we will…"

Don't start by referring to yourself. Instead focus on the content of the session (WIIFT).

In a recent article from LERN Magazine, a publication of the Learning Resources Network (http://www.lern.org) "many course descriptions lose readers before they even start. Do not start your descriptions with any of the following:

- In this class…

- Students will…

- You will learn…

- This class is…"

Bio

Don't forget to toot your own horn. One paragraph about what makes you an expert should be the last item of your description. What is it about you that a student would want to attend your class? This is advertising copy, not your resume.

REPLY POSTCARD

This is optional, but we have found that in an unsolicited submission that about 2 percent will contact us that they are interested in our program(s). However, of that 2 percent, 80 percent of them will return the reply postcard rather than call our 800 number, fax us or call us. This tells us that they are just too busy to even follow up on what they are interested in. Some schools have taken two years to contact us!

Below is a sample of a reply postcard. If you only have one class that you are proposing, try testing your title. Use 3-4 different titles for the same program and see which one draws better.

Sample Postcard

Please send us a full description/proposal for following program(s):
☐ How To Create A Successful Web Site
☐ How To Double Your Income Through Speaking
☐ Eliminate Clutter and Get Organized
☐ Time Management Through Organization
☐ Consult Your Way to a 6-Figure Income
☐ Inventing for Money
☐ Start A Successful Home-Based Mail Order Business
☐ Surfin' the Net: Using the Internet for Business and Pleasure

Name:_____
School:_____
Address:_____
City/State/ZIP:_____
Telephone/e-mail/fax:_____

If you'd like to learn more about this venue, check out the Learning Resources Network (http://www.lern.org). Virtually all of the directors of continuing education programs belong to LERN and they gear a lot of their programs to what the organization is currently recommending.

GOOD NEWS-BAD NEWS

For as wonderful as the Rubber Band venue sounds, it's not without its problems. The best part, of course, is that marketing and promotion costs are virtually zero since the school handles all of the advertising through its catalogs and related efforts. This means that whatever you receive, less the actual out-of-pocket expenses you incur are pure profit for you to keep and use.

However, just because your program is listed in the catalog doesn't mean that you'll have hundreds of attendees or even enough to make it worthwhile for you (and the school) to hold the class.

After eighteen years of operating in this venue, we know three things for sure:

1. We have no idea of what's going to be a hot topic nine to twelve months from when we propose a new program.

2. Most of the popularity of this venue comes from what's currently being promoted on TV, radio, and the print media.

3. What's hot is hot and what's not is not. When a topic, no matter how valuable it is goes out of popularity, you'll find your enrollment dwindling–fast.

The class sizes go up and down, cancels out completely, and then come back in different areas. This is typical of everything we've seen in the Rubber Band Circuit. In the past four years, our average size of class (number of students per class) has been 9.25; average number of seminars given has been 171 per year; an average of 23.5 percent of classes cancelled.

A lot of speakers and trainers who make their money solely from fees don't like the small classes because they don't make as much from the program as they do when they have a lot of attendees.

But before you cancel a class, look and see if it's potentially worth your while to hold it for a small number of students based on the potential for getting consulting clients. If the answer is yes, you'll make a few dollars, prevent the school from having to refund all of the money they've collected, and become a hero to the small but dedicated band of attendees who will appreciate that you came out to teach them regardless of the class size.

Statistically, larger groups yield less consulting clients percentage wise than small groups. We attribute this to the fact that in a smaller group, you can be a lot more focused and devote more time and attention to each individual. Even if you don't actually spend more time with each person individually, it often seems that way because of the closeness and personal nature of the interaction process.

Small groups can be extremely lucrative if you take a more enlightened approach. If you're geared to make a lot of your money from the referrals and consulting work you obtain from lecturing to a group, you'll have an intimate setting to prove that you're better at doing what they want to do than they are, and have an opportunity to demonstrate that it might be more expedient to hire you instead of attempting to do it themselves.

For example, Mike uses the charitable donation technique in his classes and offers free consultation to the attendees. In his larger groups, he rarely gets anyone to accept the offer but in the smaller groups, he gets people to meet with him and closes about 25 percent of them as clients for his services.

He once delivered a six-hour seminar for four attendees and closed $6,000 worth of consulting business. Considering that he was paid $150 for the class plus $80 for the materials ($230 total), he walked away with $6,230 in business with a zero marketing cost.

EVALUATION

Many schools and all seminars companies use evaluations or feedback forms as a way of gauging the reaction of the attendees.

Look over their form before you begin. If the form uses "on a scale of 1-10" two or three times in your seminar, where you are giving your best information, say to the group "on a scale of 1 to 10, how would you rate that" A 10! Then, when they start to fill out the forms, they will "recall" giving you "10s." If their form uses "on a scale of better to best" use that phrase instead of "1-10".

In a one- to three-hour session, the evaluation form should be short. Keep it to five questions or fewer. Make it look concise and easy to fill out. Make the evaluation forms less than a full page.

Use short answers for all but the last question(s), which can be open-ended. Quick answer questions can be yes/no or a rating scale: 1-10. One of the best uses of the evaluation form is for referrals or quotes that you can use in your promotional materials.

Sample Evaluation Form

Your evaluation of the presenter and the program is very important. It will help us to improve our programs and serve you better. We review each evaluation, so please consider each question carefully. Thank you.

Overall, were you satisfied with the program? ❑ Yes ❑ No

Check your response to the following questions: 1 poor to 10 very good

THE PRESENTER:	1	2	3	4	5	6	7	8	9	10
Understood the subject matter.										
Was well prepared for each session.										
Stimulated discussion and involvement within the group.										
Was interesting and informative.										
Provided individual help when needed.										

What did you like about the program?

What improvements would you like to see in the program? Do you have suggestions for future programs?

Do you know of any organization that is looking for a speaker? If so, do you have information on who to contact?

Can we quote you? ☐ yes Can we use your name? ☐ yes

Name:_____
Address:_____
City, State, ZIP:_____
Phone:_____e-mail:_____

What you are most interested in are the positive comments that could be used in your media kit and any referrals that people may have for you. If you don't ask, it won't happen.

RESOURCES

Here are some addresses for getting started on the Rubber Band Circuit:

Directory of Public Vocational Technical Schools by Media Marketing Group. Look for it in the reference section of the library.

For a directory of colleges, universities and community colleges, go to http://www.isleuth.com.

The reference section of your library will have several directories of post-secondary schools.

You can get a complete list of all the colleges in California (http://www.cccco.edu) and contact them about doing programs at their facility.

For a directory call *California Colleges and Universities*, write or call for a copy ($6.50) of the Guide. California Post-Secondary Education Commission, 1303 J St Ste 500, Sacramento, CA 95814 916-445-7933 http://www.cpec.ca.gov.

For a directory called State of California Adult Education Schools, Programs, and Personnel, write or call California State Consortium for Adult Education; 22100 Princeton St, Hayward, CA 94541 916-322-2175.

The following addresses are for some of the larger companies and schools that have a well-received and profitable program. Even if you are halfway across the country, these schools would be worth your while to contact.

Boston Center of Adult Ed
5 Commonwealth
Boston MA 02116
617-267-4430 x 715
http://www.bcae.org/

Chandler-Gilbert Community College
Continuing Education
2626 E Pecos Rd
Chandler AZ 85225
480-732-7000
480-732-7090 fax
http://www.cgc.maricopa.edu/

Colorado Free University
1510 York St
Denver CO 80206
800-333-6218 or 303-399-0093
303-399-0477 fax
http://www.freeu.com

Discover U
2601 Elliott Ave Ste 4215
Seattle WA 98121
206-443-0447
http://discoveru.org

First Class Seminars
1726 20th St NW
Washington DC 20009
202-797-5102
202-797-5104 fax

Fun Ed
13608 Midway Rd
Dallas TX 75244
214-960-2666

Glendale Community College
6000 W Olive Ave
Glendale AZ 85302
623-845-3000
http://www.gc.maricopa.edu/

Learning Annex
16 E 53 St 4th Flr
New York NY 10022
212-371-0280
212-319-1623 fax

Learning Annex
520 W Ash St Ste 110
San Diego CA 92101
619-544-9700
http://www.thelearningannex.com

Learning Annex
19 Irwin
Toronto ON M4Y 1L1
Canada
416-964-0011

Learning Annex
291 Geary Ste 510
San Francisco CA 94102
415-788-5500
415-788-5574 fax
http://www.thelearningannex.com

Learning Annex
11850 Wilshire Blvd #100
Los Angeles CA 90025
310-478-6677
http://www.thelearningannex.com

Learning Connection
201 Wayland Ave
Providence RI 02906
800-423-5520

Learning Exchange
650 Howe Ave Ste 600
Sacramento CA 95825
916-929-9200
http://www.learningexchange.com

Leisure Learning Unlimited
PO Box 22675
Houston TX 77227-2675
731-877-1981

Open University, Inc
706 N First St
Minneapolis MN 55401
612-349-9273

Paradise Valley Community College
Division of Continuing Education
Center for Business and
Workforce Development
18401 N 32nd St
Phoenix AZ 85032
602-787-6800
602-787-6805 fax
http://www.pvc.maricopa.edu/cc/

University Continuing Education Association
1 Dupont Cir Ste 615
Washington DC 22036
202-659-3130

University of Nevada Las Vegas
Division of Educational Outreach
4505 Maryland Pkwy
Las Vegas NV 89154
702-895-3394
702-895-4195 fax
http://edoutreach.unlv.edu/

Chapter 9 Self-Sponsored Seminars

Self-sponsored seminars are a seminar when you personally invest the money, advertising, promotion, etc.. You also get all the rewards. This is the speaking area where there is the highest risk because you pay for all advertising up-front and then wait for people to attend your seminar.

Ticket sales or 2-Step seminars are when you give a free presentation such as the Rubber Chicken circuit (or you might get paid) and during the presentation you mention that you have a seminar coming up next month (or at the next scheduled date—weekly, monthly or quarterly). The attendee pays prior to the seminar.

The system would be ideal if you were sponsoring a seminar each month. A friend of ours spoke on developing photographic memory. Approximately once a month, she would have a memory seminar at her home. During the year, she would go to real estate companies, auto dealerships and service clubs and give a free presentation on how to develop a better memory. At the end of the program, she would sell a couple of tickets for an upcoming program. She had their money and they were entitled to come to any program, but had to call in advance to let her know which date they would attend.

The first 2-Step seminar that Mike attended was in 1980 and promoted a leveraged buyout seminar that cost $2,000. The introduction program cost $5 to pay for the coffee and parking fees. During the program, you were dazzled by the skills of the presenter and over 30 people signed up for the full weekend seminar.

Of course, a self-sponsored seminar can be designed to be the product all by itself and assuming that you price it correctly, can be a source of a lot of revenues in return for sharing your knowledge from the platform.

LOCATION

There are meeting or community rooms available at apartment complexes, banks, car dealers, chambers of commerce offices, corporations, funeral homes, libraries, movie theatres, restaurants, and schools to host your self-sponsored seminars. Look in the yellow pages under banquets or meeting facilities.

Before booking these rooms, there are some questions to ask about the meeting location:

1. Is the meeting room easy to find? Or is it up, around and down a dark hall?

2. Are there restrooms available? Are there enough phones for people to call for messages or can cell phones be used inside the building?

3. Is the neighborhood safe?

The most common meeting location is a hotel. When calling the hotel, ask for the catering or sales/marketing department. Do not ask for reservations— they don't handle these requests. They handle sleeping rooms (the beds or racks).

The key to negotiating with the hotel is to understand where it makes its profit. Is it in meeting rooms, in sleeping rooms or by food? By knowing this, you can ask for concessions that will not cost ... much.

FOOD

The first thing a hotel will ask is if you are planning to serve a meal with the function. If you do, then the cost of the meeting room might go down.

For seminars prior to 11:00 a.m., it is almost necessary to provide coffee. In the mid 1990s, Fred Pryor Seminars eliminated coffee service from its seminars and saved $1 million per year. If you are not providing coffee, talk to the hotel to see if the restaurant can provide *to go* coffee for people that want/need coffee. Or see if the hotel would provide a coffee bar just outside the meeting room for the first hour of the seminar.

More people drink regular coffee (with caffeine) than decaffeinated coffee. Estimate about 2 to 1 regular vs. decaffeinated. If the session is after 7:00 p.m., then increase the quantity of decaffeinated. Also, the older the group, the more consumption of decaffeinated coffee there will be.

Watch the words that are used when asking for more coffee. If there is an hour for registration plus an hour of the presentation and then a break, some hotels will remove the urn of coffee and **replace** it with a newly brewed pot. If the staff replaces the coffee, you'll be charged for the urn that was dumped down the drain plus the new urn of coffee. Others will **replenish** (add additional or top off) the coffee to top off the urn, you'll be charged portionally. A typical cost of a gallon of coffee is $23.00 plus sales tax plus a service fee (19 percent).

It is customary in a morning session (before 10:00 a.m.) to provide a little something to eat—bagels, muffins, fresh fruit, juice. It is also customary to provide tea (some herbal). Soft drinks are usually not provided in the morning unless the seminar location is ritzy or the price of the seminar is very expensive.

When the attendees are registering in the morning, ask if they will be staying for lunch (even if they have paid for it). Some individuals will take the opportunity of the lunch break to call back to the office and handle the day-to-day matters, or if it is a sales group, a sales person might take a client/vendor/customer out to lunch, since they were in the neighborhood.

Allow about 1½ hours for lunch for over 60 people. There are several things that can reduce the lunchtime, but you need to work very closely with the hotel staff. To reduce serving time:

1. Choose a dessert that can be placed on the table to begin with (cookies, cheesecake, cakes) rather than desserts that need to be served (ice cream).

2. Have the hotel staff place the salad, and bread and butter on the table before the attendees arrive.

3. Finish the session exactly at the time stated.

As more and more individuals are becoming concerned about what they eat, vegetarian plates are frequently requested. With the meal selection, also choose a vegetarian plate. Many hotels are uncreative when preparing vegetarian plates; they simply remove the meat and substitute cheese.

On the registration form indicate if the attendee would like a vegetarian plate. The hotel prepares only the amount of plates requested, so watch for walk-up registrations that request vegetarian plates. Also watch that when the food is being served, if the vegetarian plate looks better than the regular plate, that attendees aren't asking the servers to switch their selection.

The hotel usually requires a final count on the meal 48-72 hours before the seminar. Hotels will prepare 10-20 percent more than requested. Check the contract for the exact number. If you guaranteed 100 people, you'll be charged for 100 meals, even if only 5 people show up. If there are 117 people, then you'll be charged for 117 meals.

Groups have personalities. There are groups where if the guarantee is 100, 100 people will attend (no more, no less). Other groups, only 75 show up. If you have the registration/seminar pre-paid, you are not out of pocket.

Other groups have a large number of walk-up (walk-in or daily) registrations. When selecting the meal, if the group tends to have a large walk-up registration, choose meals that can be stretched such as a buffet, pasta, meatloaf, etc., not steak or lobster.

At our local National Speakers Association/Greater Los Angeles Chapter meeting, we have an early bird rate (register three-days prior to the meeting), which is $10 cheaper than if your register just prior to the meeting or the day of the seminar.

For several years, we *monitored* the discount rate results. We had started out at a $5 discount. However, for the members, $5 wasn't enough of an incentive to care whether they pre-registered or not. When we got to $10 we found that it was significant enough for them to remember to register early rather than just wait until the last minute. This way, the organization was better able to calculate the number of meals, handouts to prepare and seats arrangement.

The hotel may charge for each plate that goes out the kitchen door or each plate placed at a table seat. Sometimes, a server will place a plate at a chair where no one is sitting (which you will pay for) or if someone is in the restroom when the server comes to their table, they might not get served.

You (and perhaps another individual) might want to count heads or provide each person with a ticket. It's easiest if the tickets are numbered and you pass them out. If you have ticket #98 in our hand, you know that you have 97 for meals. Then when you get the bill, check your count against what they charged you.

If you're not going to be providing food with the seminar, check the nearby area to see what eating facilities are available. You might want to provide a map and walking directions for people. Also, you might want to break for lunch at 11:30 instead of 12:00/12:30. If appropriate, inform the hotel restaurant that there will be 100 people coming in for lunch at 12:00. Some hotel restaurants have special plates for seminar attendees or have a buffet to help speed up the serving time.

If the group is small (under 30), another option is to have menus provided at the seminar and have the attendees pre-order their meals at the 10:00 break and provide the restaurant with the list.

Sessions that start in the afternoon (1:30/2:00/2:30) typically don't need any kind of refreshment. Or perhaps provide coffee or a little piece of hard candy to keep them awake. It is also typical to provide soft drinks in the afternoon.

MEETING ROOM

When scheduling a meeting room, there are several questions to ask, in addition to the basics (whatever those are to you).

1. What type of walls does the meeting room have? Meeting rooms with air (moveable) walls provide for greater flexibility but air walls are not soundproof. If there is a meeting in the next room—set up the seminar so the back of your room is touching the common wall.

2. How high is the ceiling? A 7-foot-high ceiling is great for a small group. However, a larger group (100+) with the presenter using a platform and a screen, the people in back can't see (and may request their money back).

3. Are there any other events being held at the hotel that day (what number)? If a large group is in the building, sometimes it is more difficult to get the attention of the hotel staff. Also, your attendees might get lost in the shuffle. The more activities going on that day, the less flexibility your seminar has. Watch the serving of food. If your seminar and their seminar sit down at exactly the same time, there might be a delay with hot food.

4. Are there any pillars, posts, or low lighting fixtures? No matter what their layout says, reduce the number of chairs. People still can't see behind a pillar.

5. What facilities are there for parking? In larger downtown metropolitan areas, parking can get expensive. Talk to the hotel to see if a discount for seminar functions is offered. If you are also giving the seminar in another location, price the downtown metropolitan seminar $5-$10 less than second locations. People may expect that you pay for their parking. At that point, you can explain that if they had chosen the other location, they wouldn't have had to pay for parking and the price was reduced because of the parking. Does the hotel own the parking or do they contract the services? If they own it, they have greater flexibility with prices.

6. Another detail to consider in the seminar location is the signage for the seminar. Frequently, the hotel will simply take your company name off the signed contract and put it on the sign-board/daily events. However, consider what the attendees remember about the seminar—and your company name might not be what they are remembering!

SET-UP

Arrive at the seminar room at least 60 minutes before the start of the seminar. Frequently, even if you have sent a layout of the room setup, the room setup is not what it should be.

If you have provided a room setup and you are doing several seminars with that setup, have the directions translated into Spanish or the language of the staff. Often times the people setting up the seminar rooms can't read English.

A common seminar style is classroom style (table and chairs). This is also the minimum number of chairs in a room. The maximum number of chairs in a room is theatre style (just chairs). For long periods of time where people are required (or want) to take notes, this style is the least effective.

Classroom Style
Seating

Theatre Style
Seating

However, once you know the minimums and maximums of the room dimensions, here's how to put this to work. A room that is three-fourths full is ideal. It doesn't look or feel empty and yet people aren't crammed in and there is room to spread out just a little.

Let's say that you are sponsoring your own private seminar. The only method of advertising is to place an ad in the local newspaper.

Free seminar on creating a successful financial future. Tuesday, January 32, 2020. Seating limited. Call to reserve your seat today. Register before January 22 and get a free gift.

Assuming the room holds 18 people classroom and 50 people theatre, if 22 people call and register, switch the seating to theatre. If there is a cancellation clause in the contract with the hotel, tie in the registration before January 22 date with the cancellation date. If you don't get your minimums, cancel. Expect between 5-10 percent no-shows. The group will vary. A free seminar would have even more no-shows.

DAYS AND TIMES

This is another one of those areas where you'll get a lot of different opinions about what times are best to hold a seminar. We've been involved with everything from 7:00 a.m. sessions to ones that start at 7:00 p.m. and none of them are any better than any other time. In reality it depends on the group you're targeting and what their schedule or availability is for the days you hold the sessions.

The most common starting times are usually 8:00 or 9:00 a.m. for morning sessions and 1:00 or 2:00 p.m. for afternoon sessions. Evening sessions can start anywhere from 5:30 to 8:00 p.m. and are usually dictated by local traffic patterns and availability of the facility. See the details below for more information about specifics.

CORPORATE SEMINARS

Monday is not a good day because people are coming back into the office after the weekend. Typically, managerial people will work the weekend and put work on associate's desks. There is also a larger volume of mail on Monday.

Friday is not a good day because people like to think that they are going to get out of the office early to start the weekend.

The last week of the month (or last month of the quarter) is not a good time if the industry has month-end close outs or quarterly reports due. The legal industry has billing that must go out at the end of the month and sales departments have commissions tied to monthly sales ending the last day of the month.

Weeks that have holidays are not a good time. People are still required to do five days of work in four days. If you ask them to be out of the office one more day, some will sign up (and pay) but not show up because of the time crunch.

Tuesdays, Wednesdays, and Thursdays are the best overall days.

A 9:00 a.m. start with an ending at 4:00 p.m. is good if the person attending the seminar works 8:00 a.m. to 5:00 p.m. 9:00 a.m. looks like they can be late compared to a normal day. The reality is that that extra hour gives the attendee the time to fight morning rush hour traffic and get lost a couple of times before the seminar starts. Typically, registration will start at 8:00 a.m.

If you are dealing with managerial individuals, then you can start the day earlier (7 a.m. or even 6 a.m.). Also, if the training is conducted over several days, it is possible to use the weekends. Attendees with small children or children in school don't have as much flexibility.

GENERAL PUBLIC

Monday evenings are not good (especially in the fall) because of Monday Night Football. If you are designing a program/seminar that would be 99.9 percent non-football watchers, it might be okay to try. Super Bowl Sunday might provide an opportunity for non-bowl watchers to do something!

Wednesday evening in many communities is church night. Friday evening is *date* night, family night and a religious observance. If you are providing an entertaining session, Friday night might be good.

Tuesdays and Thursdays are good evening weekdays and based on results, Saturday from 10:00 a.m. to 1:00 p.m. is the best single seminar time for seminars.

7:00 to 10 p.m. is a common evening seminar time. If you are planning a seminar in a time zone where you do not live (or have not lived) find out what time the late local news is on. In California, the late local news typically starts at 11:00 p.m. and in the Midwest are to starts at 10:00 p.m. The media know that people are just getting ready for bed at this time. So end your seminar so they will be home for their normal bedtime routine.

Saturday 9:00 a.m. to 12 p.m. is a good time for seminar attendees. Again, watch their age and if they have children of soccer, football, or basketball age, then Saturday afternoon might be a little better.

EXCEPTIONS

Daylight Savings Time: watch the starting time of a seminar the first week of Daylight Savings Time. People become uncomfortable with the day getting darker so quickly—especially if they are unfamiliar with the seminar location (campus or hotel).

If your attendees are entrepreneurial and run their own small business, a seminar in the afternoon is good. Although they have assistance with the business, they may not trust them to open or close the business.

If your attendees have school age children and are the primary care givers while their spouses work, a seminar in the afternoon is good. They can squeeze in the seminar while the kids are at school, and still be home for dinner and the evening activities.

If your attendees are elderly, a seminar in the afternoon is good. Many elderly people (whatever elderly is) are uncomfortable driving at night.

Sponsoring your own seminars can be very lucrative and exciting. Watch your expenses closely or it might not be lucrative.

Chapter 10 Professional Speaking as a Career

This is a unique area to consider because the industry only exists in the minds of meeting planners and the handful of directories that service the profession like the Who's Who of Professional Speaking from the National Speakers Association (http://www.nsaspeaker.org).

If you doubt this, look in your local yellow pages under professional speakers or speaker. Chances are you'll find speakers rebuild and repair; automotive radios and stereos-sales/service; speakers wholesale; speakers manufacturers; musical instruments-dealers; speakers dealers; and equipment rental and leasing but the category professional speaker is missing. However, professional speakers account for hundreds of millions of dollars in revenues each year.

SPEAKERS BUREAUS

Bureaus are an interesting enigma for people starting out in the speaking profession. You probably need them most when you're first starting out and that's the time they won't work with you. By the time you've established a mature career and don't really need them, they're anxious to do business with you.

Confused, are you? Don't be. Once you understand how they operate you'll have a much better appreciation for your relationship with them. Bureaus are a form of search firm that locates speakers and trainers for meeting planners who are looking for speakers and trainers, are willing to pay for them, and prefer to let an outside organization (like a bureau) find them a speaker. This may be a little simplistic but it'll make life easier if we keep to the basics.

First, last, foremost, and above all else, bureaus work for the people paying the bills, the meeting planner, not the speaker. The speakers and trainers they represent are the commodity and as such, are treated as a resource in a card file or database.

Here's how the bureaus work:

1. They actively market their services (not the speakers they represent) to prospects like meeting planners, associations, corporations, etc.

2. When a meeting planner decides that a particular type of speaker is needed for an event, they may decide to let a bureau do all of the recruiting, auditioning, and negotiating.

3. The meeting planner contacts the bureau with the requirements including topic, fee ranges, dates, locations, and other pertinent logistic elements.

4. The bureau then locates speakers that they feel will satisfy the meeting planner's needs and collects promotional material from the speakers including video demo tapes, copies of articles the speaker has written, testimonials, current fee schedules, and availability for the dates in question.

5. The bureau then decides on three to four of the speakers and forwards the media materials to the meeting planner for review.

6. The meeting planner then selects the speaker or speakers they prefer.

7. Once the meeting planner has decided on a speaker, the bureau issues two contracts: one to the meeting planner for the full fee of the speaker and one to the speaker that states that in return for having located the speaking engagement that the bureau is entitled to retain 25 percent of the speaker's fees.

8. Depending on the event, the organization, or their preferred level of involvement, the meeting planner may or may not contact the speaker directly for questions, surveys, and customization.

Pay special notice to the following:

1. The bureaus do NOT actively market speakers or trainers. Their function is to stand in the middle of a supply and demand process.

2. Bureaus generally look at their database of speakers and trainers that they personally know as the candidates that they refer to the meeting planner.

3. The bureaus get 25 percent of the speaker's fees. Therefore it's in the bureaus best interest to get the meeting planner to hire the most expensive speaker that meets the meeting planner's needs.

4. When you're hot, you're hot, and when you're not, you're not! When an individual gets a lot of notoriety for something (like Norman Swarzkopff in Desert Storm), they become a hot commodity, everybody wants to book them, and they can command top dollar fees.

5. Bureaus like to work with speakers who are hot, now! If you're not hot because of a topic, event, or reputation, they're probably not going to be all that interested in you.

6. Beginning speakers are generally not of interest to bureaus because they do not have an established reputation. This would require that the bureaus actively promote them, a task that the bureaus simply aren't equipped to do.

7. Beginning speakers simply don't command the top fees that experienced speakers do.

8. Beginning speakers are a potential liability to the bureaus because of their lack of experience and the fact that the bureau has probably never seen them perform. Because their reputations are at stake, bureaus don't like to refer or book speakers they don't know.

All that having been said, bureaus are a wonderful source of found money because most experienced speakers have found that their cost of sales (what it costs to get a booking) is over 50 percent. Simply stated, a $5,000 speaking engagement will cost you $2,500 in advertising, promotion, and marketing costs. On the other hand, a bureau only charges you $1,250, so it's financially expedient to have as many bureau bookings as possible.

OK, so do you get involved with the bureaus? (Don't say you haven't been warned!) Here are some resources that will give you a more comprehensive overview of how bureaus operate and how to use them effectively.

1. There is a set of audiotapes available about how to work with bureaus. They were recorded by Susie DeWeese and can be purchased from her by calling 310-230-2242. Susie owns a bureau called Speakers Corner, an excellent bureau, and she explains on the tapes, in plain language, what the bureau's role in the speaking profession is all about.

2. You can also get another set of audiotapes recorded by Dottie Walters of the Walters International Agency (http://www.walters-intl.com) at 626-335-8069 entitled "Everything You Ever Wanted To Know About Working With Speakers Bureaus But Were Afraid to Ask".

3. If you want a list of bureaus, go to http://www.IGAB.org (International Association of Speakers Bureaus) and do a bureau search. (Hint: to get all

of the bureaus in the database, search for the letter "e" because EVERY bureau name and description has a lower case "e" in it.)

4. If you subscribe to Dottie Walter's Magazine, Sharing Ideas, (http://www.walters-intl.com) at 626-335-8069 she'll give you a list of all the speakers' bureaus as a free gift. (That makes it worth the price of the subscription alone!)

5. Different bureaus specialize in different areas of expertise and different kinds of speakers. For example, some only handle religious speakers while other handle only big name celebrities. If you're smart, you'll call every one of them and ask them the following questions:

   • What type of speaker/topic do they handle?

   • What fee ranges do they handle?

   • What industries do they specialize in?

   • What materials do they want you to provide for consideration?

After you've made contact, stay in touch with them every 90 days or so by sending them a postcard, flyer, or some other piece of material so they know you're still alive and actively involved in the profession.

An excellent item to send them is your current speaking schedule. This will help convince the bureaus that you are actually working and will give them a reference base to work from. If you're going to be speaking near a bureau, invite them to hear you speak (taking them out for a meal and getting to know them socially at the same time is highly recommended since they are going to be promoting you).

As you start to contact the bureaus you'll discover that they're about as easy to speak to as opening a hole in a mountain with a pocketknife. Every time we've heard bureaus address a group of professional speakers, they wax eloquent about how and when to contact them, when not to contact them, what and what not to send them, and a myriad of other rules and regulations that appear confrontational to the speakers who just want the bureaus to notice them.

Pay special attention to the fact that the bureaus stand in the middle of the meeting planner, their requirements, the speakers, and their skills and knowledge on a particular topic. Both of these are real people, not machines, and they have two responsibilities:

1. Sell the meeting planner on their expertise and ability to locate the best speaker(s) for their event and

2. Locate speakers and trainers who can help them achieve their objectives.

Let's make it even simpler—part of the time they're selling their skills to the organization that they report to and part of the time they're buying the services necessary to make it happen. In other words they're functioning in both purchasing agent and marketing roles and they MUST divide their time between the roles to be successful. Consequently, they're not available most of the time to talk to you or have you promote your skills to them even though they might need you sometime.

Because of the complex nature of this relationship, bureaus had gotten a bum rap for trying to be in service to all the parties involved while maintaining a professional posture and fairly representing and servicing the needs of all the parties.

The bottom line on all this is to not take the indifference of bureaus towards your skills personally. They simply have a priority of their own that may or may not coincide with yours.

AGENTS

Merriam-Webster's defines an agent as: one who is authorized to act for or in the place of another as a representative, emissary, or official of a government.

A speaker's agent is a horse of a different color and our definition of a speaker's agent is: a speaker's agent is a person or organization that actively promotes a specific speaker to a potential meeting planner for a fee.

The operative phrase here is *specific speaker* which differentiates the agent from the bureau because the bureau is looking for a speaker to fill a meeting planner's needs and usually doesn't care who the speaker is. The exception to this is when the meeting planner specifically requests that a bureau obtain the services of a particular speaker.

Whether your agent operates totally on your behalf or not is a business decision that you'll get to make based on the overall proficiency of the person you hire and train.

Agents are usually hired directly by a speaker to look for opportunities for them to speak and the speaker pays the agent directly. The agent's compensation may be salary, hourly, commission, bonus, or a combination of any or all of these.

This is the exact opposite of working with a bureau because the speaker is paying for the direct efforts of the agent, whether the agent finds them work or not. What is being paid for are the efforts and not the results.

Agents may be either exclusive to a particular speaker or they may represent an ensemble of speakers. Agents may also represent keynote speaker's only, trainers only, or may specialize in a particular target market, such as a given industry or a specialty topic area such as sports celebrities.

Using an established agent might be a great idea if you can find one that meets your standards, understands your topic and your marketplace, fits your budget, and really wants to handle you. If you put all of those requirements in a cup and shake them up, you've got about as much chance of winning the lottery as you have of finding a pre-qualified agent to handle you profitably.

Most of the successful speakers we've known have failed their way to success by hiring and firing several people until they finally found one that they could work with and who would put up with the idiosyncrasies of both the profession and the speaker.

This is a marketing effort and a numbers game, pure and simple. Lots of cold calls, surveys, qualification sessions, follow up, rejection, and general nausea are involved in finding a potential meeting planner who you can even send a proposal or a media kit to.

Agents assist in negotiating fees, developing program topics, making travel arrangements, establishing an expense reimbursement program, allocating audiovisual resources, establishing and maintaining contact with the meeting planners, and generally being a wet nurse to both the meeting planner and the speaker. In other words, it's not as simple as it sounds.

This is one of the places the speaker does not work alone. You and your agent must be a team or the relationship and the efforts are doomed to failure from the onset. Here's what we have found to be the MOST effective way of getting an agent:

- Precisely define your area of expertise in terms of topic and its benefits.

- Decide who your target market will be.

- Get a list of the organizations that you believe will most likely be a candidate to hire you to speak to their people on the topic you've defined.

- Create a set of qualification questions to ask the people you are going to call.

- Create a telemarketing script.

- Conduct the qualification questions via telephone YOURSELF to prove that the system works.

- Close the deals yourself.

- After you've defined a system that works for you, hire someone to clone your system and turn 'em loose.

- If you feel that no one can close you like you can close you, have them turn the hot prospects over to you for additional conversations, sending materials, and actually closing the deal.

After you've proven that the system works to your satisfaction, you can begin to have the agent following up, sending out media kits, and eventually closing the deals for you.

If you're confident that they can handle your entire process, let 'em run with it but do check up on them occasionally to make sure that everything is being done the way you need to have done. Don't forget, you're the one who has to perform and whose reputation is on the line.

Be careful not to overload the individual too soon. We've blown out several people over the years by expecting too much from them at the start. The speaking business is tricky and time consuming. Voice mail, answering machines, and the ability to hide from people calling has made it difficult to contact prospects and it's a frustrating job to stick with it until you actually connect with someone.

The ultimate key to success lies in persistence and consistency in your efforts. If you agree that success in marketing is strictly a numbers game, then you'll have to agree that both bureaus and agents are a part of your marketing mix and at the end of the year, when you check your bank account, you'll find that they've all contributed to your economic growth.

If you want more information about pursuing a career as a professional speaker, we refer you to the *Professional Speakers Marketing Handbook*. (http://www.RoundsMiller.com). This 400+ page book on CD ROM will give you a complete picture of the speaking profession with hundreds of resources for locating bureaus, agents, associations, mailing lists, and complete details on how to approach each of the different venues to get booked.

RESOURCES

You're not alone in your efforts–thousands of professional speakers have already broken ground and there are a lot of support companies ready to assist you in your marketing efforts. First, there are several newsletters and resource sites that will be invaluable to you in the business:

SpeakerNet News–a FREE weekly on-line publication whose contributors are speakers and trainers http://www.speakernetnews.com.

Great Speaking is an electronic magazine for presentations skills tips, speaking for money, referrals, speaker marketing, speaker humor, training, and speaking related features http://www.antion.com/ezinesubscribe.htm.

Complimentary speaking and presentation skills newsletter—help for speakers of all levels http://www.fripp.com/newsletter.html.

Basics of presentation skills
http://www.mapnp.org/library/commskls/presntng/basics.htm.

Speaking resources including links to other sites, articles about speaking, software suggestions, PowerPoint templates and more http://www.school-for-champions.com/speaking/resources.htm.

Use humor in speaking plus a link to a comedy coach's web site
http://www.profitguide.com/howto/article.jsp?content=1170.

This site including motivational quotes and motivational posters
http://www.themotivationalspeaker.com/publicspeaking/.

Speaking newsletter http://www.nosweatspeaking.com/.

National Speakers Association (NSA), 1500 S Priest Dr, Tempe AZ 85281, 480-968-2552 http://www.nsaspeaker.org. It has been said that joining NSA will reduce your learning curve by 5-7 years.

American Society of Training and Development (ASTD) is an organization for corporate training. They have local chapters in most major cities. Contact ASTD at 800-628-2783.

Institute of Management Consultants (http://www.imcusa.org) is a not-for-profit, national professional association founded in 1968 to set standards of professionalism and ethics for the management consulting profession. Institute of Management Consultants, 1200 19th Street NW Ste 300 Washington DC 20036-2422, 202-857-5334 or 800-221-2557, 202-857-1891 fax http://www.imcusa.org.

Toastmasters is a great organization if you are interested in learning how to deliver great presentations, easily lead teams and conduct meetings, give and receive constructive evaluations. Toastmasters was developed to help people get over the fear of public speaking. There are over 8000 club so there should be one near you and can be contacted at Toastmasters International, PO Box 9052, Mission Viejo, CA 92690 949-858-8255, 949-858-1207 fax http://www.toastmasters.org/.

SpeakerMatch's on-line list of active speaking engagements can become your greatest booking resource. You can browse the list based on location, event dates, response deadlines, and more! $49.95 per month SpeakerMatch.com http://www.SpeakerMatch.com.

A excellent book for speakers is *New Speak and Grow Rich*, Dottie and Lilly Walters, Walters International Speakers Bureau, 18825 Hicrest Ave, Glendora CA 91741 626-335-8069 $16.95 and shipping.

How to Create and Market Speaker Products, Dottie Walters and Mike Ferry, Walters International Speakers Bureau, 18825 Hicrest Ave, Glendora CA 91741 626-335-8069 8 cassette album $125 and shipping.

Encyclopedia of Associations published by Gale Research check with your library.

National Trade and Professional Associations and Labor Unions of the United States and Canada. New York: Columbia Books, Inc., annually. Provides information on national trade associations, labor unions, professional, scientific, and technical societies and other national organizations.

Marketing With Speeches and Seminars, Miriam Otte, Zest Press, 8315 Lake City Way NE #139A, Seattle WA 98115-4411 206-523-0302 or 206-523-1013 fax $6.95.

Here are some sites that have trainer games (some free–some fee) for speakers and trainers to enhance your presentations.

Create Your Own Adventure Public Broadcast System. PBS provides a free madlib creation service. http://www.pbs.org/kratts/crazy/madlibs.

A free program that creates web-based crossword puzzles in seconds http://www.EclipseCrossword.com.

A clever technique for inserting specific user defined words or names into a pre-configured story. Elibs Elibs: An on-line service providing a place to create and post elibs. http://www.eLibs.com.

Game-O-Matic Center for Language Education and Research at Michigan State University http://clear.msu.edu/dennie/matic.

Eight free on-line programs (30 day demos) that make interactive web-based games based on users' input Gameshow Pro Web LearningWare Inc. Interactive game show style games can be created and publish to the internet or company intranet http://www.learningware.com.

Six applications to create interactive games for the web. Free of charge to nonprofit-institutions.   Interactive   Games   Interactive   Games http://www.oswego.org/staff/cchamber/techno/games.htm.

Create and host six different types of games on-line for free. Jeopardy, Who Wants to be a Millionaire, and Hollywood Squares TeachNet.com http://www.teachnet.com/lesson/misc/winnergame022500.html.

Free PowerPoint templates for Jeopardy, Who Wants to be a Millionaire, and Hollywood Squares games. Multi-Q: A Question and Answer Review Game The   Tech   Connected   Teacher http://www.esu5.org/techteacher/powerpoint.htm.

A free quiz template in PowerPoint format http://www.quia.com.

QuizStar is an on-line service where users can create on-line games in battleship, hangman, scavenger hunt, and many other formats http://quizstar.4teachers.org/index.jsp.

This is a resource center offering tips, trick, software and the latest insight into techniques and technology for delivering seminars and workshops. http://www.creativekeys.net/PowerfulPresentations/pphome.html.

The   Trainer's   Warehouse–tools,   tips   and   toys   for   trainers http://www.trainerswarehouse.com.

Chapter 11 Promotional Materials

Advertising, by definition, is creating the awareness that your services exists, and sales of your services are the only reason to advertise because if you don't tell people about your services, they can't buy your services.

Even though the best ways to promote your services are sampling and products, you're still going to have to use conventional materials because you live and work in a conventional world. There are a few items that most people consider standard but other than that, nothing is standard, and as long as it works for you, continue doing it.

First, there are four critical factors to consider when deciding what to create and send to someone to get business:

1. More is NOT necessarily better. The people that you're marketing your services to are just like you—they're up to their eyeballs in junk mail, e-mail, snail mail, and ads for everything from steam powered prune pitters to self-tying shoelaces. Most of us stand in front of our microwave yelling, *hurry up* and don't have time to look at most, let alone all, of the stuff you've sent, and your prospects are just the same.

2. This is NOT like high school where the term papers with the most pages flew the farthest from the English teacher's balcony and got the best grades. This is a case of getting the most pertinent material into the hands of your prospects. Anything more than that is not only a waste of your money but tends to overwhelm the meeting planner and may actually turn out to be a negative marketing element.

3. What you send someone depends on what you're trying to accomplish. Look carefully at the variety of objectives and steps you're taking to get booked and send ONLY what's appropriate for that particular step.

   You still only get one chance to make a good first impression. We've tossed thousands of dollars worth of personal promotional material in the trash because it was poorly printed, improperly targeted, or basically, didn't work to get us booked.

Mike is one of the people who fell prey, early in his career, to buying desktop publishing software and trying to do it himself. Guess what? It didn't work! He's not good at creating promotional materials (but GREAT at marketing) and the end result reflected that lack of capability. He learned his lesson the hard way and now let's professionals who have the talent and capabilities create the promotional material that we need so he can concentrate his efforts where he has talent, not where he doesn't.

What's this entire section mean? Simple—if you're not skilled at creating your own promotional materials, bite the bullet and hire somebody who is. Period!

If you want a recommendation, contact Sheryl Roush http://www.SolidGoldMarketing.com. She's created some of the BEST promotional materials ever seen at reasonable prices.

4. The fourth caveat has to do with those who create and produce promotional material for a living. It's in THEIR best interest for you to have them design and create more materials than you really need. Whether it's good for your career or not is highly questionable. If it were your business you'd probably recommend that everybody buy more than they need, and they do too.

POSTCARDS

For as long as they've been around, as simple as they are, it's really hard to fault or improve on the good old postcard. They're inexpensive to create, print, and mail. Postcards are great for making announcements, sending out updates to schedules or programs, and just generally keeping in touch with prospects that are interested in your products or services.

- Modern Postcard, 1675 Faraday Ave, Carlsbad CA 92008 760-431-7084 or 800-959-8365; 500 postcards $125.

- NoNEG Press, 109-A Otto Cir, Sacramento CA 95822 916-391-6797 $99 for 750 4-color sided postcards. $99 750 4-color business cards.

Nancy Miller's video *Marketing with Postcards* http://www.RoundsMiller.com is an excellent resource for learning what you can effectively use postcards for and how to create them inexpensively and quickly.

ONE-SHEET

By definition, a one-sheet is a single sheet of paper, printed on one or both sides, that contains information about a person, product, or an event.

One-sheets are the basic medium of advertising for both consultants and the services they offer. For many consultants, a one-sheet coupled with a cover letter and maybe a price sheet is all they use.

Go to the National Speakers Association web site (http://www.nsaspeaker.org) and look up some speakers. Visit their web sites and see what they've done on their one-page layouts and perhaps contact them and ask them for a copy of their current one-sheet materials. Look and see what they've done. Don't copy their material but do look carefully at what they've included and how they've targeted the audience.

One-sheets contain the following information:

1. Who you are. Why would someone want to hire you, what makes you different? Include your work-related experience. If you have educational credentials, include them; however, don't lie about them.

2. What you do. What is your area of expertise, services you provide, topic titles or what programs do you give?

3. Who you have worked for—a partial (or full) listing of clients. You might want the mix to include something in your own city, something in your own state and also national. Include associations and corporations.

4. Picture of yourself.

CAPABILITY BROCHURE

A capability brochure represents a business's ability to deal with intangible problems and produce results. The format varies, depending on your profession and what you choose to include. The most important element of any marketing or capability brochure you produce is congruity.

It must be acceptable, familiar, and non-threatening to the prospect. In today's market, the one-sheet marketing piece or its first cousin, the tri-fold brochure, is extremely popular. They are short (maximum of 2 sides), easy to produce, and easy to read. The verbiage, paper quality, inks, colors, and overall look and feel of the brochure, however, will vary based on the target audience.

A small graphic design company that targets mom and pop stores will fare better by making their brochure on simple paper with a minimum of flash. Conversely, a brochure from an airline consultant who is targeting a multimillion-dollar company needs to be of a much higher quality to keep it from being thrown in the trash immediately upon receipt. However, this same upscale brochure will cause the mom and pop store to believe that they cannot afford the services of a consultant that distributes expensive advertising.

The word for success here is congruency!

RESUMES

The process of selling services hinges heavily on the written word, regardless of the actual work that is performed. The first component of a consultant's written material is a resume because all consultants need a resume in one format or another. The conventional format, however, is generally unacceptable for any kind of marketing efforts because it is completely focused on the background of the consultant.

Bear in mind that when selling, the focus must be on the client's needs and any document, such as a resume, that focuses completely on the consultant tends to detract from the selling process. A resume or statement of background qualifications is an essential component in the marketing package, but as a stand-alone marketing tool, it usually fails.

Regardless of the format used, one thing stands out in all successful consultants' resumes: all of the material is about the specific experience for that topic. It is not deceptive or fallacious to exclude non-pertinent information from this type of resume. If the client interviews you in person, in all likelihood the entire conversation will deal with the consulting topic and will never touch on other elements of your business career.

Why, then, should a resume be any different? It is simply a written chronology of those things that are pertinent in the consultant's background that give credibility to his or her credentials for performing the services under consideration.

BUSINESS CARDS

Thought and consideration should go into designing your business card since it might be the single element that a prospect keeps around for a long time and eventually uses to locate you or more specifically, what it is that you do.

The first question that people receiving your business card should be able to answer is, "What business are you in?" If you are in an industry where you, your name, and your business are all tied together, put your picture on the card.

If you are selling yourself (e.g. speaking) you should have your picture on the card because you are the product.

Beyond D is a printer that we use to print our business cards. Contact Scott Shiota at 2730 Monterey St, Torrance CA 90503, 310-212-5110 x 103 mailto@Scott@BLD.com.

TESTIMONIAL LETTERS

There doesn't seem to be any sort of consensus about what or what not to do about reference letters. We've heard them referred to as testa-balonial letters because everybody can find three friends to write a good testimonial for them and nobody in their right mind is going to send a prospect a letter that says that they're inept or incompetent. The one thing we do know is that you should ask the client for reference letters, even if you're not planning on including them with your standard promotional materials.

The basic reason for a testimonial letter is to give the prospect a warm and fuzzy feeling that they're not alone in considering your services and that their are others (that they can call) who have already used you and are satisfied.

If you want to establish your history or longevity in the industry, then include an old letter (you were good way-back then) and a current letter (and you are still good today).

There are several steps you can take to increase the likelihood of getting a testimonial letter from a client.

- In your initial contact, suggest that if they are pleased with your presentation that they write a letter to you stating their pleasure.

- The day of the engagement, ask for the letter at the point of ecstasy. "I really appreciate what you're saying. Would you be willing to write that in a testimonial letter for me?" Ask that they address the letter to "To Whom It May Concern."

- Within the next 24 hours, write a handwritten thank you note saying how much you appreciated the opportunity, how fun the group was, etc.

- If a letter doesn't arrive within two weeks, you could call as a follow-up. Be sure to mention that you are still waiting for the testimonial letter.

- Keep their business card in your pocket and when the individual walks away, jot down the words that were used.

- Listen closely at the point of ecstasy for the words the person used. If you are preparing the testimonial letter for their review, use as many of the same words as you can.

- If you are being taped during the presentation, ask the AV person to continue recording until the last person leaves the room. You can then use the person's voice and actual words later on.

- If they are pressed for time, offer to write the letter on their behalf, send the letter to them, have them edit any wording so they are comfortable with the wording, and then print the letter on their letterhead.

- If you are writing the letter, start with a grabber opening and end with a power closing and limit it to one page.

POINTS OF A GOOD TESTIMONIAL LETTER

- It is on letterhead stationery.

- Date of the meeting or when the work was performed. There is no hard and fast rule about the date on the letters. However, use the most recent letters. Anything after two years starts to be dated. Some individuals white out the date and continue to use the letter in their promotional materials. Others use *except style*, which does not utilize the date at all.

- Place of meeting or where the work was performed.

- Title of presentation or nature of the work that was performed.

- Audience size or scope of the project.

- How would they describe the audience reactions or management's acceptance and implementation of our suggestions?

- What did they like best about the presentation or working with us?

- It contains a statement in the letter about:

- If there were evaluation forms, a specific positive comment or two from the participants.

- How you fulfilled the objective of the presentation.

- What made you special or different from all the other speakers?

- Bonus: suggesting that they will be using you again in the future.

- Bonus: any reference about what you said that has now been implemented.

- Bonus: that they recommend or refer additional people for you to contact, or that they have passed your name and phone number along to other individuals.

Excerpts

You don't have to use the entire letter if you don't want to. These letters can be a great resource for accolades that you can use in your advertising materials. We've used excerpts from reference letters, as well as the good comments on the bottom of review sheets, in many of our promotional and advertising materials.

In choosing the representation for the letters, here are a few suggestions:

1. Choose an organization or company in your own city (you are an expert in your own backyard).

2. Choose an organization or company in your state (you are an expert in your own state).

3. Choose an organization or company with national representation (you're not just a local kid).

4. Choose an international organization or company (especially if you want to do more international business).

SIGNATURE AND TITLE

Instead of using the full first and last name, use only initials. With some companies (say an IBM for instance), they may not want to have their local sales manager endorsing anyone without first clearing it with in-house legal, and specialized corporate counsel.

If the contact is any good (which you hope they are), then within some period of time, they will be promoted within the organization or move onto another company. By using the initials, those that know the person personally will know who it is and those that don't won't care. With this method, the materials tend to be less dated.

Be sure to include the job title or job function. CEOs like to see what other CEOs have said about you. Meeting planners want to see what other meeting planners have said.

REPRINTS

Whenever your name is in a newspaper or magazine, you can use it in the media kit. However, just photocopying the articles doesn't look that professional alongside all the other materials. In other words, if you're gonna' do it—do it right!

Send a letter to the editor requesting their acceptance of your reprinting the article. Then in the reprint, include the phrase *Reprinted by Permission.*

Request a velox print immediately. Because a velox is a little expensive, they might not just give it to you. However, if you can get and use one, your reprints will look much better.

If you do not get a velox or don't request it, request a tear sheet and send a SASE (self-addressed stamped envelope) along with the request. Now that you have the tear sheet, if is possible to have a printer re-key the article.

Another method is to do it yourself by copying or scanning the article with dark paper behind it on the machine's lightest setting. Cut out the copy of the article (along with the main headers and sectional headers) and carefully paste it using a re-position able fixative spray-mount (which can be found at Aaron Brother stores) on blue line graph paper, exactly as the copy is to appear. Double check to be sure all lines are straight. Use white out on the marks from the newspaper and smudges from the copy machine.

Make a half tone of the photo—use photo captions, or even insert your own promotional photograph instead of the photograph taken by the newspaper. Use a white-coated stock paper to make your reprints.

DEMONSTRATION TAPES AND CD'S

If you're selling your platform skills, you'll need demonstration material. There are different styles, formats, lengths, and techniques used for creating them. It is so diverse that nobody really agrees with what should be provided or included.

PICTURES

With computers, having your picture as a jpg, bmp, wpg, etc. is very easy. There are a couple of different styles.

First there is the caricature, a comical or exaggerated picture. If your topic is fun, entertaining, etc., this style will work fine. Contact Kim Fiori, 24100 Beverly Drive, Quail Valley CA 92587 909-244-7624. Her hand-drawn portraits can be used for advertisements, business cards, profile sheets, letterhead, and logos and are artistically created from your photographs.

Second is line drawing or line art. Take your photo to Kinko's and have them scan it (if you don't have the equipment in your office). The picture at the left is actually a line drawing of Nancy Miller that was created from a photo of her. Since it's in black and white, it's faxable and reproduces well.

Ad Graphics, Jim Weems, 5829 South 81st East Pl., Tulsa OK 74145 800-368-6196 or 918-252-1103 Four-color graphic design, faxable photos, book design and one-pagers. Jim has a $99 program for the line art from a photograph. What we like about Jim is that after we got the picture back, we took a highlighter and highlighted areas where we wanted dots removed (too much of a 5 o'clock shadow) and where we wanted dots added (part of the chin wasn't there).

MEDIA/PRESS KIT ORDER

Now it's time to bring all these pieces of paper together. The media kit includes: brochure, topic sheet, schedule, fees, client letters, and product information. The topic sheet or topic description is a complete description of topic, including bulleted points and quotes from clients who used that topic/presentation.

Now that you have put all this time and effort into the kit, be sure that when mailing it the material arrives intact and presentable. Sometimes the paper envelopes do nothing to protect its contents. Pizza boxes make great shipping containers.

Pocket folders are a very popular way to conveniently package everything. They work well because you can tailor the package by simply slipping or inserting whatever materials are required for this specific client's needs into the pockets of the brochure.

To get custom folders, it will cost $1-$3 each. Many printers now have stock quasi-custom folders that give greater variety. If you decide to use pocket folders for your media kit or your proposals, remember these three things about them:

1. The materials that so easily slipped into the folder just as easily slip out and become part of a disjointed pile of material.

2. Because the pocket folder is larger than the standard piece of paper or file folder, the client will likely remove the materials from the folder and throw the folder away so that the materials fit into a file folder or filing cabinet.

3. Binding the materials together using a simple binding system or padding them with padding compound will ensure that materials that were created to be reviewed and kept as a set will stay as a set.

A SPEAKER'S WEB SITE

The web has become an invaluable tool for speakers to offer their materiel to interested parties for virtually no cost and in matter of moments. There are a few key things to consider before you construct your site:

1. The web is a gigantic library that people can access for free—anytime they want to use it.

2. Your web site is the electronic equivalent of a book. Just because you can write and electronically print a lot of material doesn't mean you should. People have time constraints so keep it short and to the point.

3. Your book is created for the reader, not for your own personal enjoyment or entertainment. Keep all the fancy graphics, animated cartoons, and other distracting elements off the site unless they're a critical part of the information.

4. Get a URL (name) for your site that makes sense. It should be uniquely yours and be something that people will remember. Do your best to keep it fewer than 15 characters or less. The longer it is, the more possibilities there are for the reader to mistype it and then they'll never find you. To find out if the name you want is available, go to http://www.WhoIs.net.

5. A linked table of contents on the home page that's easy to use is a must to make sure the reader can find what they're looking for—fast. Put it in the margins so the reader can get to it from anywhere inside the site! Make the layout logical and simple to navigate.

6. Graphics and other large files take a long time to download because of slow modem speeds. Current statistics show that 80 percent of the web's users are still using POTS lines (28.8 or 56k modems). Your home page should download in less than 10 seconds with a 28.8 modem.

7. Put your contact information in several places and make it easy to find. This includes name, address, telephone, fax, and e-mail.

8. Most people don't know how to use a search engine. The best way to get people to your web site is to use conventional advertising. Get your URL in their hands so they can go directly to your site.

WHAT TO INCLUDE

1. Home page – This is the cover of your book and where the reader (visitor) will get their first experience of you and what you have to offer. It should be clean, tell the reader who you are, what you do, and how to quickly and easily find the information that they're looking for. Additional things that should be included are: your picture (low resolution), contact information and a hot-linked table of contents to the rest of the site.

2. Program descriptions – This is what most people will be interested in. Although you can make the pages fancy remember that any graphics or clip art will take longer to download. List and link these descriptions. For example list each topic you address and then link to a page that contains short (<100 words), medium (<250 words) and long (<500 words) descriptions about each program.

3. Introductions – Having your introductions (generic and specific ones for each presentations) available from your web site will allow you to download and print them out whenever and wherever you need them. Things that should be considered are:

    *   Make the typeface large (16 point).
    *   Use a serif font (the ones with the little tails).
    *   Keep it to 100 words or less if possible.
    *   Keep it one page maximum.

4. Questionnaire – About 75-80 percent of all the customization data and logistics for most programs can be answered with a questionnaire. Post the questionnaire on the web site so the meeting planners can fill it out and e-mail or fax it back to you.

5. Bio Info – Many of the programs, organizations, and facilities you will be speaking for want to include your speaker's biography in their brochures and advance advertising documents. A page with the information you want published is a mandate for quick and easy delivery of these documents. The typical lengths are as follows: short (<500 words), medium (<100 words) and long (<200 words).

6. Graphics – Having a variety of pictures and clip art available on your site will assist the meeting planners and their layout people in getting the brochure done on time. Here are some of the things you might want to consider:

    *   Head shot black and white; low resolution (72-150 DPI JPEG).

    *   Head shot black and white; medium resolution (150-300 DPI JPEG).

- Head shot black and white; high resolution (300-600 DPI GIF).

- Full length or action shot full color; low resolution (72-150 DPI JPEG).

- Full length or action shot full color; medium resolution (150-300 DPI JPEG).

- Full length or action shot full color; high resolution (300-600 DPI GIF).

- Clip art and/or caricatures black and white line art; low resolution (72-150 DPI).

- Clip art and/or caricatures full color; low resolution (72-150 DPI).

7. Fee Structure – Although there is some controversy about making your fees available to the general public, it's a good idea to put them on your web site where they are easily accessible to those who need to see them. This page should include the following information:

   - The effective date of the information.

   - Your fees for the different types and times of speaking you offer.

   - Your deposit and cancellation policy.

   - Your travel expense and accommodation requirements.

   - What, if any, support material will be included for the participants or if it will be quoted separately.

   - Your policy regarding the audio and/or video taping of your program.

   - What books and tapes you will make available and at what discounts, if any, to the participants.

   - Your performance guarantee.

8. References – Although nobody ever gives out copies of negative reference letters, reference letters are still one of the things that clients will ask you to supply. There are several ways to post your references:

   - By industry—if you're targeting specific industries lump the reference letters from them together.

- By topic—if you've addressed specific topics, lump them together so that a meeting planner who's interested in the same topic can find them easily.
- Full copies—you can scan the entire reference letter and put it on your site for reading and printing.
- Retyping—you can retype the copy from a reference letter to create a clean and readable reprint.
- Excerpted—since most people don't have a lot of time, you can excerpt the reference letters and attribute the person and their company.

9. Professional Resume – Your speaker's bio will be focused on the topic that you currently address. Nevertheless, a full professional resume with everything is what you'll want to include with this document.

10. Articles – In addition to making your articles available for reading and reference, you should put written permission on the articles allowing anyone to reprint them as long as they give you credit and put your contact information on them.

11. Schedule – This is the one optional element for your web site. (You'll have to decide for yourself if it will help or hurt your business). If you don't have a lot of business yet, it will automatically show your lack of bookings. Conversely, if you're heavily booked it will tell the reader when you're available and when you're not. If you're doing public seminars and workshops, it's a great way for readers to see where they can see you or send people to see you.

12. Special Items – This is the "extra good stuff" portion of your web site where you can put the information you want people to have access to that doesn't fall into the other categories. Many speakers put tips for their audiences, additional notes or handouts, tests, quizzes, references, and resource documents on their sites as support items for their programs and tools for convincing prospects of the value of their programs. Make sure that you follow good layout and logical design in this section. Sub-menus and options for high vs. low resolution and long vs. short copy still apply.

13. Hidden Pages – There are a lot of things that we want only selected people to have access to and this is where we put them. These include notes, handouts, and material specifically developed for a specific group of people and not for public consumption or some form of special offer that's only being made available to selected clients. Another popular use of these pages is for material (for example an e-book) that is sold but can only be accessed by people who have been given the exact URL of its location on the site. Other items include maps with driving directions to home offices, price lists, client interaction documents, and other proprietary information. These pages should NEVER have a link ANYWHERE on the

site! The only way a reader should know that they exist is because you have given them the URL!

14. Products – Your books, tapes, videos, CD's, and other products should be posted on your web site for sale along with a shopping cart.

- Shopping cart – this is actually an order form or order blank that can sent back to you via e-mail to make it easy for visitors to order your materials and have it shipped in a timely fashion.

- Merchant account – the world buys with plastic (credit cards).

- The best bet at this time is to go to www.PayPal.com and apply for their program. It's free until you need it and their fee is about 2 percent of the transaction fee.

15. Demo Material – The ready availability of multimedia computers means that most people who use the internet can play streaming audio and video demonstration material. This is a great advantage because it saves you from having to ship videotapes all over the world plus you can put live excerpts from your programs on your site as sample material. The biggest problem is knowing the actual speed and display capabilities of your prospective clients. Here are some recommendations and options for adding this dynamic function to your web site:

- The cheapest recorder (it's free from http://www.microsoft.com) is the Windows Media Player and Recorder. With this software you can encode everything from a narrated slide show that'll look and sound good with a 28.8 modem through a DSL or cable connection with real time viewing capabilities.

- The three programs for playing streaming video are Apple's QuickTime, the Real Player, and the Windows Media Player. All three are great and the players are free. Don't forget to include a link back to the appropriate website so the visitor can download the free player software if they don't already have it installed.

A speaker's web site can be a valuable tool for you. You can develop it to meet your needs and it is ever changing.

Rave reviews for NANCY MILLER

"It was well organized and presented with enthusiasm. Sounds as if you've put into practice what you preach."
M.C., Seal Beach, CA

"Very informative and interesting. I need it, as I am full of clutter. Stimulating. Helpful!"
C.A.B., Seal Beach, CA

"Helpful hints, examples, ways to reduce clutter."
D.A., Registrar, San Diego, CA

"Interesting ... and helpful comments give hope and encouragement."
M.B., Activities Coordinator, CA

"It was very informative with good ideas for application."
L.S., Sales–Real Estate, CA

"Very informative on storage. Gave me many new ideas to reorganize my home."
J.R., CA

"It was very interesting. So much information was covered. Useful data was covered."
A.K.G., College Administrative Secretary (retired), Ventura, CA

"Loved it. A lot of good information."
K.B., Ventura, CA

"Some of the littlest things have already made a BIG difference!"
J.C.H., CAE TJ Management Group

"Nancy is a seasoned professional and adapts her talk to the areas most sought after by her audience."
S.R., Leisure World Library

"The program motivated everyone to unclutter and get organized. We have used your tips and everyone is still talking about it!"
K.P., Assoc. Petroleum Wives, Bakersfield, CA

"In short, you are SUPERB!! We have attended quite a few of her seminars on this subject but never did we have a bountiful harvest such as from your seminar!!"
J.Y. and T.Y., CA

"Thank you for your wonderful presentation. When I see members of the staff that attended your workshop, they break out in a big smile and give me an example of something they have done to "un-clutter" their lives or their work site. To me, this is a real measure of success."
J.S., Staff Development Coordinator, Pasadena, CA

Label everything (except people) so that the next time you try to find it, you can (page 90)

If you don't know what it is, toss it! (page 88)

It's easy to clean around nothing (page 51)

Chapter 12 Trademarks and Copyrights

Independent contractors, consultants and speakers are constantly involved with a great deal of intellectual property, which makes them ready candidates for both the registration of their materials under the copyright and trademark laws as well as potential violators of the rights of others under the same laws.

To effectively operate under the rules governing trademarks and copyrights, we have included information to use as guidelines. The material contained in this section is abbreviated and excerpted from a detailed section in our book *How to Sell Your Inventions for Cash*. Since the law is constantly changing, we recommend that you check out the latest rules and regulations on the appropriate U.S. government web sites as follows:

Trademarks: http://www.USPTO.gov

Copyrights: http://www.LOC.gov

TRADEMARKS

Because of the amount of advertising, promotion, publicity, and subsequent reputation that becomes connected with goods and services, trademarks tend to become the identity under which people recognize and purchase a particular line of goods or services from a supplier.

In other words, a trademark is the mark of your trade or how your goods and services come to be known and recognized. As a result, the trademark may become as valuable, or even more valuable, than the goods or services, which it represents.

Clutterology®

The clutter dude and name Clutterology® shown at the right is an example of a registered trademark. They belong to Nancy Miller, the owner and creator of the book and training program Clutterology® Getting Rid of Clutter and

Getting Organized and she, and she alone, can use these marks or authorize others to use them.

Incidentally, the registered mark includes the graphic character clutter dude the name (Clutterology), or both when they are used together.

So what are trademarks? From a practical standpoint they are a word, symbol, slogan, or even a distinctive sound, which identifies and distinguishes the goods and services of one party from those of another. Some specifics of trademarks are that they:

- Take 6 to 13 months to be granted depending on the category selected and the backlog of work.

- Are granted for a period of 10 years and are renewable, as long as the mark is maintained in an active status.

- Have maintenance fees. If the forms are not filed and the fees are not paid, the mark is considered to have been abandoned or canceled, and deprives the registrant of the exclusive right to use the mark.

- Cost $335 per submission, not including charges for the artwork, forms, etc.

- Require the filing of a form and payment between the 5th and 6th year in order to ensure they do not fall into the public domain.

- Are considered to be an asset and may be bought, sold, leased, licensed, traded, bartered, confiscated, awarded, or willed in any form of sale, legal action, trust, or judgment.

- Have 34 classes of goods and 8 classes of services under which a trademark may be registered. It is possible to register the same name in different classes of goods or services.

- May not be granted if either the name or the graphic portion of the trademark is deceptively similar to another trademark in the same category.

FILING A TRADEMARK

In order to prevent the rejection of a trademark application, you are encouraged to research trademarks that are in existence at the time of application.

The process involves six primary steps:

1. You can do a manual submission using the U.S. Government forms. To obtain them, you can go to http://www.USPTO.gov and obtain your materials on-line using the internet.

2. Review the book, Basic Information Concerning Trademarks, as it shows you exactly how to develop the artwork, how to fill out the forms, and how to submit them. It'll also provide you with a current list of product and service classifications so you'll know which category applies to your trademark.

3. Design the graphic logo and determine the name or slogan.

4. Have a preliminary trademark search run to determine if the mark you want to register is available or has already been taken.

   A preliminary search can be run by a patent agent, patent attorney or the patent and trademark room of a patent library to determine if the mark is available or taken.

   You'll find that many of the public libraries offer the trademark search service for a minimal fee. Some public libraries will perform the research, by computer, for $50 to $100, depending on the amount of on-line computer time required. It usually includes a search of federal and state trademarks.

   The federal search is inclusive from 1884 to within a few weeks of the present and is updated on a weekly basis. The file does not include those marks that were canceled (an affidavit was not filed in the fifth or sixth year), abandoned (the trademark was never published) or expired (the trademark was not renewed).

5. Place the mark, name, slogan, etc. on a product and make a legitimate sale of the product, across state lines, in exchange for money. It's mandatory that you sell a product with the mark affixed. This is defined as using the mark in commerce, and is a requirement for receiving a trademark.

   By strict definition, one usage of the mark is all that is required to comply with the letter of the law. Selling a single item with the mark affixed across state lines (interstate commerce) fulfills the requirements.

6. File the completed application, artwork, etc. with the USPTO. You'll need to provide the USPTO with five samples of the mark as it's used. A supply of samples of the mark, logo, package, letterhead, etc., will suffice.

Do not send the product!

TRADEMARK MARKS

The marks (™, SM, and ®) indicate different things:

1. The ™ (trademark) may be placed on any logo, name, slogan, etc., as fair warning to others that you are using this as your trademark.

2. The SM (service mark) is usually placed on a logo or other device for firms that are dealing with a service, rather than a product. The rights, restrictions, and cautions are the same as when using the ™.

3. The ® (registered mark) is allowed on a mark only after the mark has been officially approved and granted by the USPTO.

The, ™, SM or ® marking should be large enough to be easily spotted and should be placed as either a superscript (shoulder) or subscript (heel) immediately following the mark.

You can check the latest filing fees at http://www.USPTO.gov. Look under "file" and then "Filing Fee and Refund Policy" to see what's new.

INFRINGEMENT

Some of the more important rights accorded to a trademark holder are as follows:

1. The right to sue in federal court for trademark infringements.

2. Recovery of profits, damages, and costs in a federal court infringement action and the possibility of treble damages and attorney's fees.

3. Constructive notice of a claim of ownership.

4. Upon presentation of prima facie evidence of valid ownership of the mark, the exclusive rights to the usage of the mark as defined in the registration.

5. Availability of criminal penalties in an action for counterfeiting a registered trademark.

6. Providing a basis for filing trademark applications in foreign countries.

The trademark laws define trademark violations as being violations of the counterfeiting laws since they are a form of forgery or counterfeiting.

DECEPTIVELY SIMILAR

A mark may be denied if it is declared to be deceptively similar to an existing name or mark. It is the mark, which identifies and distinguishes the goods and services of one party from those of another.

Let's look at an example. Let's say that you have decided to market a line of batteries in the U.S. but you're going to have them manufactured in the Philippines. You know that the name Duracell (a registered trademark of Mallory) and the black and copper coloring (trade dress) are what people use as a guideline for selecting the batteries for their electronic equipment.

You decide to call your batteries Durable Cell and make the coloring on your batteries black and brown.

From a distance, or at a quick glance, the customer might confuse your batteries with the Duracell line because the names are similar and the coloring or trade dress is close enough to be confusing.

Because the customer might confuse the two brands, the mark will probably be denied especially, if it appears that the sole reason for the similarity is to confuse the customer into believing that they are buying the other trademarked item.

TRADEMARK GRAVEYARD

There is a caution or drawback regarding trademarks. A manufacturer spends considerable advertising dollars to get the name of the product in front of the consumer. If the consumers begin to use the trademark name generically, the government can withdraw the trademark. There have been numerous occurrences in our past: aspirin, elevator, kerosene, octane and even linoleum, just to name a few.

COPYRIGHTS

Wouldn't you know it, the most powerful form of protection available is both the cheapest and the easiest to obtain? It's called copyright and it gives the creator of original works of authorship the exclusive rights to make copies or to authorize others to make copies.

Copyrights are technically defined as original works of authorship including literary, dramatic, musical, artistic, and certain other intellectual works. They're automatically granted upon the fixing (creation) of an idea in fixed or tangible form.

Copyright is a form of protection provided by the laws of the U.S. (Title 17, U.S. Code) to the authors of original works. This protection is available to both published and unpublished works.

Section 106 of the 1976 Copyright Act generally gives the owner of copyright the exclusive right to do and to authorize others to do the following:

- To reproduce the work in copies or phonorecords;

- To prepare derivative works based upon the work;

- To distribute copies or phonorecords of the work to the public by sale or other transfer of ownership, or by rental, lease, or lending;

- To perform the work publicly, in the case of literary, musical, dramatic, and choreographic works, pantomimes, and motion pictures and other audiovisual works;

- To display the copyrighted work publicly, in the case of literary, musical, dramatic, and choreographic works, pantomimes, and pictorial, graphic, or sculptural works, including the individual images of a motion picture or other audiovisual work; and

- In the case of sound recordings, to perform the work publicly by means of a digital audio transmission.

If the word phonorecords is unfamiliar to you, original copyright laws were intended to cover the old vinyl records as the sole means of storing sound. The term has since come to mean virtually any form of recording device or medium that allows the faithful recording and replaying of material, either audible, visible, digital, or a combination of them.

It is illegal for anyone to violate any of the rights provided by the copyright law to the owner of the copyright. These rights, however, are not unlimited in scope. Sections 107 through 121 of the 1976 Copyright Act establish limitations on these rights.

In some cases, these limitations are specified exemptions from copyright liability. One major limitation is the doctrine of fair use, which is given a statutory basis in Section 107 of the 1976 Copyright Act.

In other instances, the limitation takes the form of a compulsory license under which certain limited uses of copyrighted works are permitted upon payment of specified royalties and compliance with statutory conditions.

For further information about the limitations of any of these rights, consult the copyright law or write to the Copyright Office (http://www.LOC.gov).

SECURING A COPYRIGHT

The way in which copyright protection is secured is frequently misunderstood. No publication, registration or other action in the Copyright Office is required to secure copyright. There are, however, certain definite advantages to registration.

Copyright is secured automatically when the work is created, and a work is created when it is fixed in a copy or phonorecord for the first time. Copies are material objects from which a work can be read or visually perceived either directly or with the aid of a machine or device, such as books, manuscripts, sheet music, film, videotape, or microfilm. Phonorecords are material objects embodying fixations of sounds (excluding, by statutory definition, motion picture soundtracks), such as cassette tapes, CDs, or LPs. Thus, for example, a song (the work) can be fixed in sheet music (copies) or in phonograph disks (phonorecords), or both.

HOW LONG DO COPYRIGHTS LAST?

The answer currently is the life of the author plus 70 years.

Copyrights can be registered with the government (although there are other ways to do it), cost a mere $30 filing fee for each application, and the protection is available to both published and unpublished (not yet released to the world at large) works.

You can get all the information you need to file your own copyrights, including the forms, from the Library of Congress at http://www.loc.gov/copyright/. In addition, http://www.benedict.com is a support web site that has a wealth of information, forms, and services that will assist you in the copyright process.

WHAT RIGHTS ARE COVER OR PROTECTED?

Copyright protects original works of authorship that are fixed in a tangible form of expression. The fixation need not be directly perceptible so long as it may be communicated with the aid of a machine or device. Copyrightable works include the following categories:

1.   Literary works. Literary copyrights are the most familiar for many of us. Look for the copyright notice whenever you open a book. It's usually listed on the backside of the title page or at the bottom of handouts or on brochures in the margins.

2.   Musical works, including any accompanying words. This includes MP3, compact disc, cassette tapes, and phonographic records. Everything from music-on-hold, elevator music, music in the malls, radio stations and even music in the gym is policed primarily by two organizations,

ASCAP (American Society of Composers, Authors and Publishers http://www.ascap.com) and BMI (Broadcast Music Incorporated http://www.BMI.com). BMI operates as a not-for-profit organization. They represent more than 180,000 songwriters, composers, and music publishers with 3,000,000 works in all areas of music. BMI distributes royalties to its songwriters, computers, and publishers, for the public performance and digital home copying of their works. BMI keeps track of local radio broadcasting, noncommercial college radio, and television feature, theme and cue music performed on networks, cable TV stations and local TV stations.

3. Dramatic works, including any accompanying music. This category includes scripts, stage plays, poetry, operas, and related works of an artistic nature. It includes dramatic works, including any accompanying words, like plays and screenplays. Most professional screenwriters and playwrights always file copyright on their work before exposing it to the public.

4. Pantomimes and choreographic works. These works include the dance routines for major theatrical productions like Cats, A Chorus Line, Les Misérables, the routines of mimes, cheerleader routines, or the Radio City Music Hall Rockettes Dancers. This category also includes football and basketball play books where the moves and actions of the teams are pre-organized or choreographed by the coach for the sole and exclusive usage of the team they coach. For a team member or other person to copy and distribute those plans is a violation of the copyright laws and makes the person who copies the material liable for both civil and criminal prosecution.

5. Pictorial, graphic, and sculptural works. This category includes photographs, cartoon characters, and maps. Other familiar items that are covered under this section of copyright include plush dolls (known as soft sculptures), advertising banners and posters. For example, computer programs and most compilations are registered literary works, whereas maps are registered as pictorial, graphic and sculptural works.

6. Motion pictures and other audiovisual works. Audiovisual works include videotapes, DVD's and motion pictures. Motion pictures are audiovisual works consisting of a series of related images which, when shown in succession, impart an impression of motion, together with any accompanying sounds. They are typically embodied in film, videotape, or videodisk. A number of individuals contribute authorship to a motion picture, including the writer, director, producer, camera operator, editors, and others. Sometimes they are jointly listed as the creators of the copyrighted work and sometimes they are not. The

reason that all the individuals involved in creating one of these works may not be listed on the copyright as authors is because a motion picture or video production is frequently Work-Made-For-Hire.

7.   Sound and video recordings include live, unedited tape or camcorder recordings. This has been greatly expanded to include film, digital pictures, and MP3 recordings. As new methods of recording and playback are developed, they will, by their very nature, be included under this heading.

8.   Architectural works. An original design of a building embodied in any tangible medium of expression, including building, architectural plans or drawings are protected under copyright law. The work includes the overall form as well as the arrangement and composition of spaces and elements in the design but does not include individual standard features or design elements that are functionally required. For example, a building is a structure that is habitable by humans. It is intended to be both permanent and stationary, such as houses, office buildings, churches, museums, gazebos, and garden pavilions. It's look and the design components that go into it are copyrightable materials.

These categories should be viewed broadly. For example, computer programs and most compilations may be registered as literary works; maps and architectural plans may be registered as pictorial, graphic, and sculptural works.

NOT PROTECTED BY COPYRIGHT

Several categories of material are generally not eligible for federal copyright protection. These include among others:

- Works that have not been fixed in a tangible form of expression (for example, choreographic works that have not been notated or recorded, or improvisational speeches or performances that have not been written or recorded).

- Titles, names, short phrases, and slogans; familiar symbols or designs; mere variations of typographic ornamentation, lettering, or coloring; mere listings of ingredients or contents.

- Ideas, procedures, methods, systems, processes, concepts, principles, discoveries, or devices, as distinguished from a description, explanation, or illustration.

- Works consisting entirely of information that is common property and containing no original authorship (for example: standard calendars, height and weight charts, tape measures and rulers, and lists or tables taken from public documents or other common sources).

INFRINGEMENT

Like trademark violations, copyright infringement is a form of forgery, the theft and/or usage of someone else's property.

The general principles are as follows:

1.   Mere ownership of a book, manuscript, painting, or any other copy does not give the possessor the copyright.

2.   The law provides that transfer of ownership of any material object that embodies a protected work does not of itself convey any rights in the copyright.

3.   The owner of copyrighted material may make archive copies of the copyrighted material for personal usage. These copies may not be loaned, sold, distributed, rented, or otherwise transmitted to any person or company other than the owner of the copyrighted material. If the copyrighted material is sold or transferred, all archival copies must accompany the copyrighted (original) material.

Case law in this area is pretty scant because of the economic realities of litigation. Copyright infringement doesn't usually become an issue until someone has made some serious money off someone else's creation.

DERIVATIVE WORK

Because copyright is granted to the author of original works of authorship, it's important that any research work you do prior to actually embarking on what you consider to be original work, be approached judiciously.

If you aren't careful, the work you do may be construed as derivative work, and declared to be the property of the original copyrighted work from which you obtained your inspiration. Only the author, or those deriving their rights through the author, can rightfully claim copyright.

The following examples show some of the many different types of derivative works:

• Television drama (based on a novel).

• Motion picture (based on a play).

• Novel in English (a translation of a book originally published in Russian).

- Drawing (based on a photograph).

- Books of maps (based on public domain maps with some new maps).

- Lithograph (based on a painting).

- Drama about John Doe (based on the letters and journal entries of John Doe).

COPYRIGHT NOTICE ELEMENTS

> © 2006 Mike Rounds All Right Reserved

A copyright has four elements. They are:

1. The term copyright. The © (c in a circle) notice is used only on visually perceptible copies. Certain kinds of works—for example, musical, dramatic, and literary works—may be fixed not in copies but by means of sound in an audio recording. Since audio recordings such as audiotapes and phonograph disk are phonorecords and not copies, the © (c in a circle) notice is not used to indicate protection of the underlying musical, dramatic, or literary work that is recorded.

2. The year of copyright. This is the year of publication.

3. The name of the copyright holder. The legal owner of the copyright is not necessarily the author or creator of the work. Works created by employees in the course of their employment or independent workers who sign Work-for-hire Agreements are considered to be creating the work on behalf of the employer. In these works the copyright is vested in the person doing the hiring.

4. And the phrase All Rights Reserved.

FAIR USE

Fair use provisions of the copyright law allow for limited copying or distribution of published works without the author's permission in some cases. Examples of fair use of copyrighted materials include quotation of excerpts in a review or critique, or copying a small part of a work by a teacher or student to illustrate a lesson. New issues about fair use have arisen with the increased use of the internet.

Fair use is determined by:

1. The purpose and character of the use, including whether such use is of a commercial nature or is for nonprofit educational purposes.

2. The nature of the copyrighted work.

3. The amount and substantiality of the portion used in relation to the copyrighted work as a whole.

4. The effect of the use upon the potential market for or value of the copyrighted work.

Generally speaking, quotes are considered fair use when less than 250 words are used from one source, like a book or feature length article. Short nonfiction pieces, poems, and songs are different because of their length and you should request permission regardless of how much you use.

WORK-MADE-FOR-HIRE

Although the general rule is that the person who creates a work is the author of that work, there is an exception. The copyright law defines a category of works called Work-Made-For-Hire. If a work is made-for-hire, the employer and not the employee is considered the author. The employer may be a firm or organization or an individual.

Section 101 of the copyright law defines Work-Made-For-Hire as:

1. A work prepared by an employee within the scope of his or her employment; or

2. A work specially ordered or commissioned for use as a contribution to a collective work, as a part of a motion picture or other audiovisual work, as a translation, as a supplementary work, as a compilation, as an instructional text, as a test, as answer material for a test, as an atlas, if the parties expressly agree in a written instrument signed by them that the work shall be considered a Work-Made-For-Hire.

Examples of works for hire created in an employment relationship are:

*   A software program created by a staff programmer for a computer company.

*   A newspaper article written by a staff journalist for publication in a daily newspaper.

- A musical arrangement written for XYZ Music Company by a salaried arranger on its staff.

FILING A COPYRIGHT

To register a work, send the following three elements in the same envelope or package to:

Library of Congress
Copyright Office
101 Independence Ave SE
Washington DC 20559-6000

1.   A properly completed application form (http://www.loc.gov).

2.   A nonrefundable filing fee of $30 for each application.

        Note: Copyright Office fees are subject to change. For current fees, please check the Copyright Office web site at http://www.loc.gov/copyright, write the Copyright Office, or call 202-707-3000.

3.   Non returnable deposit of the work being registered. The deposit requirements vary in particular situations. The general requirements follow. Also note the information under Special Deposit Requirements.

        a.   If the work was first published in the U.S. on or after January 1, 1978, two complete copies or phonorecords of the best edition.

        b.   If the work was first published in the U.S. before January 1, 1978, two complete copies or phonorecords of the work as first published.

        c.   If the work was first published outside the U.S., one complete copy or phonorecord of the work as first published.

        d.   If sending multiple works, all applications, deposits, and fees should be sent in the same package. If possible, applications should be attached to the appropriate deposit. Whenever possible, number each package (e. g., 1 of 3, 2 of 4) to facilitate processing.

Index